GAMES AND PARTIES
FOR ALL OCCASIONS

GAMES AND PARTIES
FOR ALL OCCASIONS

by JAMES W. KEMMERER
and EVA MAY BRICKETT

BAKER BOOK HOUSE
Grand Rapids, Michigan

Copyright 1962 by T. S. Denison
& Co., Inc.

Paperback edition issued by
Baker Book House
  First printing, July 1974

ISBN: 0-8010-5347-1

Library of Congress Catalog Card Number: 61-18650

CONTENTS

1 — Games for Special Occasions 7

2 — Circle and Line Games 31

3 — Relays and Races 45

4 — Miscellaneous Contests 53

5 — Trick and Mystery Games 65

6 — Charades and Stunts 82

7 — Games for Little Tots 86

8 — Songs for Group Singing and Musical Games 90

9 — Skill Games 105

10 — Choral Speaking 116

11 — Suggestions for Party Costumes 119

12 — Suggestions for Successful Parties 122

13 — High School Parties 124-200

CHAPTER ONE

Games for Special Occasions

Topsy Turvy Party:

On the party invitations announce that boys must attend in girls costumes and that the girls must dress completely in male clothing. No masks except domino to be worn, the boys to furnish the food and serve it. The prizes for the best dressed boy and the best dressed girl may be obtained by having each person make an original creation in advance of the party, something made by their own hands, and to be judged by disinterested persons during the party. Each creation will then be awarded to the opposite sex according to the ranking merit for the handcraft and costumes.

Hobo Party:

Persons or groups with limited money may appreciate a simple party without elaborate costumes. The name "Hobo" may be substituted for "Poverty" or another desired name, with announcements made on penny postcards. For a Hobo Party all furniture should be removed, including rugs, with an imitation campfire created in the center of the room, stories told around the fire, and refreshments served on the oldest or most battered dishes obtainable. After the lunch each person should be required to wash his own plate, cup and other utensils. Or the party may be conducted as a poverty social with a nominal fine for jewelry or new clothing worn. The invitations may be worded as follows:

Come to our .... party; Come one, come all,
(Name)

To be on .... for the short and tall;
(Day and hour)

The fat and slender, the young and old,
The meek and boisterous, the calm and bold.

*A *New Year's Party* we will give
In clothing patched on pants and sleeve.
Those who come in garments new,
At the door will not get through.

Come in tatters! Come in rags!
Come in homespun,—burlap bags!
Make up your face,—have on a mask,
Is all your host and hostess ask.

----

*Name may be substituted.

New Year Reverie:

Make scrap books for each guest or one book for a definite number of players. These may be made from wrapping paper with the pages tied together with cord string. Divide each book into chapters which deal with either community or national events. Have each individual or group make a pictorial history from magazine clippings. Example for chapter headings on National Events: "Political Events," "Industrial Happenings," "Important Persons," "The President," etc. For individual history the following subjects should be included: birth, babyhood, childhood, games or interests, college or school days, first love, first defeat or disappointments, expectations, marriage and other items. The subjects should be such as to create humorous situations. Provide old magazines, scissors and paste. Display books after completion.

New Year Resolutions:

Provide guests with pencil and paper. First, instruct each person to write a name at top and fold the paper over as to conceal the writing, and to pass the paper to the next person. Second, have each write a resolution, fold the paper and pass it. Third, the reason for the resolution. Fourth, the means by which the resolution will be kept. Fifth, the only condition under which the resolution will be broken.

After each statement has been written, the paper should be folded and passed. Upon the completion of the fifth statement the papers are passed again. Then each is unfolded and read in turn.

New Year Stunts:

New Year stunts may be built around various subjects. The following are suggested: Historical events of the past year; dramatization of a song appropriate to the occasion, as "There's A Long, Long Trail," "Comin' Thru the Rye," etc; an old timer's program,—old people singing old songs, dancing or playing instruments outmoded,—melodian, old-fashioned accordian, etc.

An effective conclusion may be the dramatization of Father Time, with a secluded reader rendering "The Last Leaf," (*Oliver Wendell Holmes*), followed by a small child in diaper and flowing sash,—draped from the right shoulder to the left hip,—the child distributing candy kisses. The sash may have inscribed upon it, "Happy New Year 19......." A familiar song may be the final activity.

Famous American Shrines:

Provide questions on slips of paper for the guests to answer. Set a definite time for this game, as five to ten minutes.

QUESTIONS	ANSWERS
1—Where is the Cradle of Liberty?	Boston, Mass.
2—Where is Benjamin Franklin's home?	Philadelphia, Pa.
3—Where is Concord Bridge?	Concord, Mass.
4—Where is Plymouth Rock?	Plymouth, Mass.
5—Where is George Washington's tomb?	Mt. Vernon.
6—Where is the Betsy Ross house?	Philadelphia, Pa.
7—Where is George Washington's birthplace?	Williamsburg, Va.

QUESTIONS	ANSWERS
8—Where is the Gettysburg Battlefield?	Gettysburg, Pa.
9—Where is the Lincoln Memorial?	Washington, D. C.
10—Where is Independence Hall?	Philadelphia, Pa.
11—Where is Valley Forge?	Valley Forge, Pa.
12—Where is the Statute of Liberty?	New York Bay.
13—Where the Smithsonian Institute?	Washington, D. C.
14—Where is the Hall of fame?	New York City.
15—Where is the Washington Monument?	Washington, D. C.
16—Where is Grant's Tomb?	New York City.
17—Where is Lincoln's birthplace?	Near Hodgensville, Ky.
18—Where is the Lincoln home?	Springfield, Ill.
19—Where is McKinley's Tomb?	Canton, Ohio.
20—Where is Old South Church?	Boston, Mass.

Pass the Hatchet:

Cut either from red construction paper or colored cardboard a hatchet. If cut from construction paper, another hatchet should be drawn on and cut from plain cardboard and the construction paper mounted on it.

Form the players into a circle. At the beginning of the piano music the hatchet is passed from player to player. The person having the hatchet when the music stops must drop from the game. The same applies to any player dropping the hatchet.

This game may be adapted to "cut-out" cherries, a colonial hat, or any object in keeping with the occasion. The game may be played as a relay. (See Relays.)

Cherry Pie Contest:

Old stunts often cause a hearty laugh. Bake a cherry pie, leaving pits in cherries. At the table place four plates with a quarter of a pie in each. Select four persons to eat the pie and four persons of the opposite sex to feed the pie to the eaters. Place bibs around the eaters, seat them at their places at the table, and at the given signal have the "feeders" begin feeding the "eaters." All pits must be deposited on the plates, none on table or floor. And no "eater" must touch the pie with his hands. The couple finishing first must pick up any pits that may have fallen, clean crumbs from the table, and fold the bib by the plate before being permitted to announce the finish.

Getting Acquainted:

Cut out either small hatchets, colonial hats, or full-sized cherries from red construction paper. Cut only one item, either hatchets, or colonial hats, or cherries. After these have been cut out, cut them into two sections, placing one section in a box for the boys and the other section in a box marked for the girls.

At the beginning of the party line the boys in one row and the girls in another row, each facing the other. At a given signal each takes the part of a hatchet from his or her opponent, introducing themselves as they do so. The director then gives another signal and the players find partners by matching the part of the object in his or her hand. When a partner is found the boy and the girl must exchange the given and surname with the other.

Presidents:

A pleasant diversion is to hang the pictures of the Presidents about the room with their names omitted or covered. *With pencil and paper each person or group writes down on his pad the name of each President according to the number on the picture. The player or team having the highest score wins the game.

Presidential Quotations:

Select famous quotations from Washington *and Lincoln. Each player or group writes down the author in numerical order as the game leader reads each quotation.

Presidential Birthplaces:

Select as many birthplaces of the Presidents as desired and conduct the game as above.

Presidential Parties:

For a *real* mental teaser ask the political parties of ten Presidents.

Various Paper and Pencil games related to the Presidents may be constructed from an Encyclopedia or a history book.

NOTE: By adapting the materials or subjects to the occasion, the foundations of the games listed on pages 12 and 13 may be used for games for other special parties or seasons. Much fun and personal satisfaction results from building original games.

Valentine Post office:

Cut out hearts from various colors of paper, one for every person present. Pass the hearts. Then instruct everyone to write some valentine greeting and his name at the bottom.

Have each player pass the heart to the third person to his right, and to deposit the heart in the "Post Office" box in the center of the room. After all valentines have been deposited, blindfold a player and have him draw out one at a time, while another player reads each, including the author's name.

This stunt will afford much fun.

This game may be adapted to birthday, Christmas, New Year's and other parties in which greetings are appropriate. For other occasions use a seasonal item, as an imitation birthday card, a "cut-out" Christmas bell, etc.

Pass the Heart:

See "Pass the Hatchet," Page 12, make a cardboard heart to pass, and follow the game accordingly.

Getting Acquainted, Valentine Party:

This game, which has been adapted from "YES AND NO",* may be used for all occasions by adapting it to the specific party or play period. (See footnote.)

For a Valentine Party have an equal number of hard inscribed candy hearts for each guest. "Yes" and "No" are two forbidden words, neither of which can be used without a penalty. At a given signal the guests begin moving about, conversing with others, hoping to cause each person contacted to say "Yes" or "No." Every time the forbidden word or words are used, the person using "Yes" or "No" must forfeit a candy heart to the person with whom he is talking. The player having the largest number of candy hearts at the conclusion of the appointed time wins the game.

Game Building:

By carefully studying the games already given and those which follow it will be observed that definite patterns or foundations underlie games as truly as certain foundations support buildings. Why not try building original games? The fun involved will fully compensate all of the concentration and effort required, and your guests will appreciate your ingenuity if you can present to them a few good games of your own making.

St. Patrick Song Fest:

Sing old songs, as: *"Believe Me, If All Those Endearing Young Charms;" "The Wearing of the Green;" "When Irish Eyes Are Smiling,"* etc.

One or more of the songs may be dramatized on the stage or in an especially constructed frame, about seven feet high and as wide as necessary, trimmed in green, with a clay pipe on each side cut from bristol board or white paper.

Items peculiar to any one party or season may be used, including small seasonal favors, other candy, marbles, toothpicks, etc. (See *"Forbidden Words."*)

*Author Unknown.

Shamrock Relay:

See "Pass the Hatchet," Page 12, and follow instructions using shamrock cut from bristol board, covered with green crepe paper or painted. Green construction paper may be used.

Irish Sayings:

As a means of getting acquainted, prepare slips of paper with Irish sayings, leaving enough space at top and bottom for a person's name after the paper has been cut diagonally from corner to corner.

Pass out sections to guests. Have each person write his name on his section, then find the person who possesses the section belonging to his.

The wider the variety of quotations the more successful this game will be.

April Fool Party:

Suggestions for an April Fool Party do not necessarily imply an evening filled with practical jokes or fun at the expense of others. One secures ample criticism, and is sometimes laughed at, in his work. Why not build a program in which all may laugh together? The following activities may be built into a very wholesome party.

1—A MASQUERADE BALL OR PARTY.

2—A FASHION SHOW reviewing all of the male and female outmoded attire available, requiring all persons to come to the party wearing their costumes and dominoe masks.

3—A FOOL'S PARTY in which the guests are invited, previous to the party, to come dressed as clowns, dunces, or other foolish characters desired. A small prize may be awarded to the person with the best "make-up," and another small prize to the person remaining in his or her character the best.

Humorous Band:

In advance of the party, select people to form a band using an ensemble of kitchen ware or other items which will cause a laughable situation, as:

Bass Drum ....a dish pan or basin.
Cymbols ....two kettle lids.
Leader's Baton..........wooden rolling pin, meat cleaver, etc.
Accordian ....toy reproduction or collapsible hat rack.
Fife ....long knife sharpener.
Snare Drum ....frying pan.
Trombone ....sliding curtain rod.
And other improvised instruments according to desire.

A regular band or orchestra may be secured, and be placed in a secluded position, to carry on from a definite point. Or both the humorous and the real band may play together so as to cause the guests to wonder how the music is created. For the most effective results, the actual musicians should be off stage or in another room immediately behind the Humorous Band.

A variation may be to secure an orchestra in which one instrument will fall apart at a strategic moment, or during an instrumental solo. With a little practice this stunt can be carried very effectively.

Humorous Singer:

Secure a talented singer to impersonate a highly opinionated amateur singer who, when reaching a very high note, makes very *sour* music. Her voice may break completely, while in the rear, off stage or in another room, an equally talented singer carries on as the first singer looks about in embarrassment or concludes the stunt in a duet with the secluded singer.

Backward Spelling Bee:

Consult "Spelling Bee", Page 64, and follow that game pattern. Have the players spell the words backward. The player spelling down the others wins the game.

Spider Web:

Instead of the traditional Grab Bag, stretch and intertwine cord strings from one room to another with a gift at the end of each string. Have the guests trace out a string apiece. Suspend strings from the ceiling.

Easter Egg Relay:

Make an equal number of line bases with pieces of paper along two sides of a room, one line each for each team. Place on each base a colored egg. Choose teams with captains. Provide each with a basket, and at a given signal the captains begin picking up the eggs, placing each in his basket as he hurries to the other end of the line. As soon as he has picked them up another person on his team takes the basket and begins laying down the eggs until reaching the head of the line, whereupon another person begins picking up the eggs again. Both teams continue this process until all persons on each team have participated. The team completing its work in the shortest time wins.

Jelly Bean Relay:

After choosing teams with a captain each, spread an equal number of jelly beans along a line for each team. With a cup in hand and a spoon the captains take the lead in picking up each bean with a tea spoon, placing it in a cup without touching another bean in line with the bean or spoon with which he is working. This relay continues the same as above.

Easter Egg Hunt:

This traditional sport always pleases. Either in the house or on the grounds place colored, chocolate, and china eggs. Jelly beans may also be used. Provide each person or group with a basket. At a given signal the hunt begins. The person or group finding the largest number of good eggs, which may be either colored or chocolate, wins the hunt.

Rabbits:

The players are formed in groups of "fours", as rabbit pens, with a fifth person in the center as a rabbit. The object is for the two extra persons who are "IT" and are children seeking the Easter Rabbit, to tag a rabbit running from one pen to another. Each person caught becomes a part of a rabbit pen and forfeits an Easter egg to the pursuers, and a *child* becomes a rabbit. As forfeits are paid each egg is placed in a common basket. The last person caught wins, and the game concludes with the last two children sharing with the group the Easter eggs from the common Easter basket.

(For the possibilities of a host or game leader building original games see, in conjunction with this game: *Babes in the Woods, Cluck,* and *Rats.*)

Duck and Geese:

Two players are in a circle of interlocked hands. "IT", the blindfolded partner, as Rachel in *Jacob and Rachel,* may employ various ruses to avoid being caught. The game begins with the circle turning and all crying, "Quack! quack!" When "IT" cries, "Quack! quack! the circle stops and he tries to catch his unblindfolded partner. When he catches him that player becomes "IT", is blindfolded, selects a partner to pursue by pointing his finger at a player after he has been blindfolded and the circle has turned again. If he is pointing at space instead of a person, the circle gives the goose call, turns and stops at his command until he has pointed directly at a player. That person enters the inside of the circle, and the game continues as before.

A variation may be to have but one person on the inside of the circle, who is blindfolded, and attempts to identify a player, between circle turnings, by feeling the hands and asking that individual to quack either loudly or softly. (With this game, study *Jacob and Rachel* and *Store.*)

Trolley Ride:

This activity, which was developed from the familiar Progressive Dinner, may be given various names if adapted to other transportation conveyances.

In advance of the party invitations or announcements should be mailed. These in themselves will arouse curiosity. Second, arrangements should be made for persons serving specific lunch items in their homes, and in some places permission to play games. Third, secure a secretive person to be the Trolley Conductor. He should be provided with a cow bell or other improvised gong. Lastly, an extra room at the place of meeting should be prepared for the first stage of the journey. Utmost secrecy should prevail regarding all plans and the program.

After the guests have arrived they are blindfolded in small groups and led into the extra room by special conductors. No more than one person beyond the game leader should be in on the secrets of the extra room before the party starts. Various well known vacation places or cities, natural wonders, shrines, etc., may be represented. A suspended pail filled and dropping water slowly, so as not to damage clothing or make persons wet,—merely enough to cause sensation when passing under—may represent Niagara Falls or the Johnstown Flood. Pieces of wood covered by a heavy mat may represent the Rocky Mountains. Damp cloths suspended on a line but far enough apart so as not to swipe the person over the entire face, may be Natural Caverns. The last stage may be Buffalo, where two persons are engaged in pouring water from one pail into another. Four pails are required. After the persons have been finally led to the place near the running water, a paper bag is burst as the conductors cry, "Buffalo!" No station is announced until the blindfolded persons have passed through each improvised station. As each group finishes the journey in the darkened extra room, those persons are seated along the wall and another group is led through. As the last group is making the journey fares are collected and preparations made for the journey through the community. Where possible, all doors are locked toward the street and an exit is made through the back of the building.

When all is in readiness the instructed conductor makes an unnoticed exit, begins ringing his trolley gong and crying, "All Aboard! All Aboard!" He does not permit all of the players to be out of the building before he starts running and ringing his gong. The first jaunt should be equivalent to at least two city blocks or squares, where the conductor stops and enters the first home. Throughout the various journeys either the game leader or some appointed person who knows where to go, should remain midway between the straggling groups. Where the group is large it is well to have another instructed person farther back. At the first house bouillon and wafers may be served and games played afterward. During the games the conductor obtains instructions from the game leader where to stop next. When interest is high he slips out unnoticed and begins calling and ringing his gong as previously. The rush of the group, so as not to be left behind, may be comparable to a center rush in football. At the second stop salad may be served and a quiet game played before starting for the third objective. Some activity should be in process each time the signal to be going is announced.

At the third stop the meat and vegetable course may be served with a beverage. If the distances are great, a fourth home may be made the objective for playing quiet games. Here the beverage may be served instead of with the meat and vegetables. The fifth stop may be for dessert and the final beverage. The last jaunt is back to the place of meeting for disbandment.

Any group seeking an active all-evening party should try this activity. If all plans are kept secret, the continuous injection of the unexpected will keep curiosity and interest high to the finish, and the young people will beg to have the party repeated. Once the Trolley Ride is tried by an organization it is certain to become an annual affair.

NOTE: Persons with weak hearts or serious physical ailments should not participate. This is a very strenuous activity.

Vacation Party:

It is often difficult to get much done during vacation months. Further, unless the weather is cool at the time of the summer party people do not care for strenuous activities. While one may find ample material in public libraries for summer parties this program will prove very interesting.

The following outline is suggested for any summer month. Jumble the important words in the invitation as here illustrated.

THE .... MEETING will be at ....
        (Month)   (Place and Time)

Mr. Fish will speak on Cavanignito—(Vacationing).

Mrs. King will give a report on Mumers Krow—(Summer Work).

The Dnoiccroa Dnab will nishruf uicsm—(The Accordian Band will furnish music).

Lunch will consist of Danwsishec—(Sandwiches),
    Trifu Dalsa—(Fruit salad),
    Eci Mearc—(Ice cream),
    Ekac—(Cake),
    Garvebsee—(Beverages).

This party may be anything from a display of sportsmen tackle to pictures or lectures on vacationing. If the weather permits the average person enjoys the out-of-doors. An accordion or string band could keep interest high with cowboy music and songs which the audience join. A quartette in cowboy costumes would also add spice.

May Day Festival:

Select a prominent girl of the community or organization to be crowned as the May Queen. Construct a throne, May pole with streamers fastened to the top of the pole, and secure persons to perform the May dance around the pole. An orchestra, vocal music and one or two speakers may be secured to support the festival. This may be either a social or money-making project. Games and refreshments may be featured after the crowning ceremonies.

Pre-Nuptial Party:

Old love songs may be sung, a fashion show of old-time bridal costumes, or former brides and bridegrooms posing or wearing their wedding clothes for display, or a Tom Thumb or a mock wedding.

Folk Festival:

Have an out-door or lawn party with folk dances, special music, games, a stunt or short play featuring the customs and costumes of a period of American or foreign life, concluding with refreshments.

Folk songs may be featured: plantation, cowboy, boat, and other early American songs afford a wide selection for a colorful program if sung by persons who are dressed in the costumes of the period or craft from which the song arose.

Hallowe'en Silent Supper:

The guests are seated around a dining table. Lights should be very dim or entirely off. One individual, who has been previously informed, begins passing the following objects under the table, whispering to the person to whom he passes the articles what each is supposed to represent: a few skinned grapes are dead men's eyes, a damp sponge a human brain, a hair transformation the scalp, a wet glove and a silk stocking filled with wet sand the hand and foot, a rabbit's foot the dog's leg. Before the game starts, instruction should be given to carry on the conversation in a whisper only.

Auto Accident:

The above game may be varied by having the players blindfolded and required to accept each item from the hand of another player as the game leader relates a gruesome story of an auto accident.

Hallowe'en Ghosts:

On the party invitations instructions may be given for each person to appear in a ghost costume. For the first part of the party the lights are dimmed and ghost stories are told before a fireplace or imitation fire. The imitation fire should be constructed with a light bulb, and fire wood covered with red crepe paper. A prize may be offered for the most gruesome tale.

The Witch's Cats:

Prefixes and suffixes afford real "mental teasers" for paper and pencil games. The prefix "CAT" is used as an example for game leaders who may wish to build original games from the dictionary. Ten or more words should be selected with a common prefix and suffix, and a poem or dialogue built to include each word.

The Game:

After paper and pencils have been passed, the Witch arrives, calling "Kitty! Kitty! Here, Kitty!" as she looks behind and under furniture. A guest, who has been informed in advance, may begin the conversation with her in similar manner: "What are you seeking, old Witch?"

WITCH. "I'm looking for my cats."

GUEST. "Your cats? Have you lost any?"

WITCH. "Yes. I've lost every one and can't find them."

GUEST. "Well, that's too bad. May we help you find them?"

WITCH. "Do you know their names?"

GUEST. "No. But with your aid we may learn them."

WITCH. "All of them begin with 'CAT,' C-A-T." *(She spells word.)* "The first one is an old tom cat. Many's the time he has kept me awake at night with his yell that sounded like he was saying, 'A log! A log!' So I named him after his yell. *(Answer.)* CATALOGUE.

"Another acts like a mountain lion. I named him accordingly. CATAMOUNT

"One was always wanting soup. So 'Soup' became his name." CATSUP

The dialogue may continue with the use of the following words: CATASTROPHE,
    CATEGORY,
    CAT-O'-NINE-TAILS,
    CATECHISM,
    CATACOMB,
    CATARRH,
    CATERPILLAR, etc.

By eliminating the witch and the dialogue this game may be adapted to any occasion.

The Witch's Brew:

A very successful stunt was carried out by a woman who had acted as the Hallowe'en Witch for many years. Instead of the traditional booth for fortune telling she had a shelter made of boughs in the darkest corner of the hall. In the front she made an open fire with a small light bulb, red crepe paper over wood, having a small electric fan to add effect. Over the fire was suspended a small round antique iron kettle. In this she had a special tea streaming by the means of an electric water heater placed in the kettle. Against the shelter was a rough bench upon which she and her black cat sat. Here she carried on a monotone conversation with herself or the cat. Her conduct coupled with her facial makeup and costume, against the weird shelter, made young and old feel "creepy". The number of people who refused to drink her brew was amusing. But the proceeds from her fortune telling paid a large share of the party expense.

In each community are persons desiring an outlet for their dramatic talents. The wise recreational leader will note and use these persons with the same care as his games. If some of these people will cooperate with him but once a year, it is better to use them where they can express themselves the best than to coax them into various dramatic programs where they cannot express themselves adequately. One stunt well done is better than a dozen poor ones produced by persons participating only to satisfy the director.

Getting Acquainted, Thanksgiving Party:

Provide the players with paper and pencils, and instruct them to make a name record of the guests present from the word THANKSGIVING. Example:

T—Thatcher, Mary
H—Harris, John
A—Andrews, Philip
N—Noll, Carrie
K—Knapp, Harry
S —Snyder, Ralph
G—Goodrich, Alfred
I —Ingram, Bessie
V—Vries, Marian
I —Isenhower, Richard
N—Nottingham, Paul
G—Greer, Elliott

This game should not be played unless the game leader is positive the name record can be built from the names of the persons present. After the pencils and paper have been passed the players are to obtain signatures from the guests in the order given. The person or group completing the record first wins the game.

Thanksgiving Dinner:

A variation of the above game is to divide the players into groups and to have them build a dinner menu from either the word DINNER or TURKEY. This is not as easy as it may seem. Example:

D—Dates
I —Ice cream
N—Nape of Venison
N—Nuts
E —Elk Roast
R —Relish

Thanksgiving Menu:

Another paper and pencil game may be made by placing well-known food advertisements about the room. The trade-marks or names on the advertisements are cut off or covered. The players are supposed to make a menu mentioning the brand, as Del Monte peaches, Campbell's soup, etc., according to the numbers appearing on the advertisements. The advertisements are cut from magazines.

Know Your Advertisements:

By cutting advertisements from magazines various paper and pencil games may be built, and adapted to any occasion. A central theme should be considered, as: Health, Food, Luxuries, Sports, etc.

Thanksgiving Tableau:

Colorful stunts are the most appreciated. Why not build a Harvest background for the musicians: corn stalks either in shocks or separate, with pumpkins, apples in baskets, in the foreground, or turkeys painted on paper and mounted on easels? Singers costumed as Puritans may stand by the turkeys and produce a very pleasing effect.

Second, tableau the Landing of the Pilgrims. Plymouth Rock may be constructed by tying two willow boughs into arches, bending each bough and tying the ends, and fastening both together with light twine at the intersecting arches. See Illustration (Fig. I) below. Lay a tarpaulin over the frame.

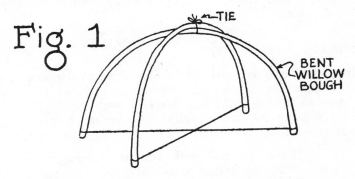

Sound effect for the rolling surf may be obtained by rubbing two pieces of sand paper together slowly back stage.

Third, other scenes may be The Pilgrims Going to Church, taken from the painting thereof, and The First Thanksgiving

Dinner: either a hunting scene or both Indians and Pilgrims seated at a rough table.

Music appropriate to the place and the occasion should be selected for each scene. Readings may be made back stage from the Masters.

Costumes:

Costumes may be inexpensive. Hats may be made of colored or white bristol board covered with black crepe paper. Cuffs may be made from white bristol. Silver buckles may be cut from cardboard and covered with tin foil or silver paper. Ladies' costumes may be made by securing old-fashioned full dresses, using white handkerchiefs for three cornered shoulder scarfs, handkerchiefs pinned to hair or small bonnets for head dress. See a history book or pictures in city library for suggestions in costuming. Here ideas for scenes may also be obtained.

All house and stage lights should be subdued. If the lines of costumes and faces are cut too clearly by the lights, the effect will be lost.

Other Costuming Effects:

For other dramatic occasions cheese cloth may be used because it is inexpensive and may be easily dyed in practically any color desired.

Christmas Carol Party:

Invitations may be made by folding common stationery into four sections like commercial greetings and invitations. Draw on the face an old-fashioned fireplace with logs aglow and stockings hung for St. Nicholas. On the inside print from "Deck the Hall":

> "Deck the hall with boughs of holly,
>   'Tis the season to be jolly,
> Don we now our gay apparel,
>   Troll the ancient yuletide carol
> At the home of ....
>   (Name of hostess)

....

(Day and date)   (Time)

As the guests arrive give each person a section of a well-known carol printed or written on slips of paper, as:

Sages, leave your contemplations,
Brighter visions beam afar,

from "Angels From The Realm of Glory." Break up each carol into couplets,—two lines to a person,—and at an appointed time have each individual find the persons who have the rest of the carol. The group who is able to assemble their carol correctly in the briefest time wins the game.

Or pass out slips of paper with a verse of each carol being jumbled line for line as,

Bethlehem town of little O
Still thee lie we how see
And deep sleep thy above dreamless
By stars the silent go
Dark yet shineth in thy street
Everlasting light the
All the hopes the years and fears
Tonight are met in thee.

The persons or group being able to find those players having the other verses of their carol and to rewrite the whole correctly wins the game.

Christmas Grab Bag:

Have an undecorated evergreen tree. Either prior to the party, or during the game period when the guests are engaged, lay wrapped gifts upon the branches. Each package should have a long cord string attached to it and hanging from a branch so that it may be pulled at the proper time. Strings should cross each other and be so intertwined that the individual pulling a string could not be certain as to which package it belongs. A member of the recreational committee should stand by the tree with scissors in hand to cut the strings and take off the packages. This will prevent strings from becoming tangled.

A group wishing to raise money for the needy poor, so as to provide toys and other Christmas gifts, may charge a set price for each string pulled. The grab bag may be used as a gift exchange for the group, each person purchasing a gift to be placed on the tree.

Santa's Bag:

Instead of the Grab Bag as a means to help the worthy poor, a pre-appointed Santa may stand near the door for the arriving guests to drop designated gifts into his bag. All gifts should be in wrapping paper as they came from the store. The specific needs of the poor families should be learned in advance of the party through a special committee appointed to contact each family, or to otherwise learn their needs. After the guests have arrived, the gifts are sorted and wrapped in Christmas paper ready for delivery. The committee may meet in advance of the party and secretly allot definite articles to be purchased by certain members.

Christmas Folk Festival:

The membership may be divided into groups in advance of the party, each group being instructed to perform a definite Christmas stunt, either through dramatization or a description created by the persons to whom the feature has been allotted. By careful preparation the dramatization of Christmas in Other Lands may provide a very unique and pleasant evening, especially if the dramatization is done in costumes.

One group may dramatize Christmas in England: the early morning carol singing and bringing in the Yule log.

Other customs possible of dramatization are:

France with its *Pere Noel,* Father Christmas, visiting children with rewards and with Ruprecht who carries switches.

Holland, where the children clean their wooden shoes and fill them with oats and hay for St. Nicholas' white horse, and their shoes being filled with gifts and candy.

Denmark, with its kind Brownie, *Nisson;* a small, old man with a long gray beard.

Norway, with the sheaf of wheat fastened to a pole near the house, children placing their shoes outside the house, and trimming their Christmas trees.

Germany, with Ruprecht visiting homes prior to Christmas and asking whether children have been good. If the children have been good, he throws nuts about from his bag. If they have been bad he leaves a switch.

Spain, the three Wise Men acting as Santa Claus.

Italy, the appearance of Mother Goose, *Befana,* on her broomstick; the lighting of the Christmas log; a large urn filled with gifts; children singing or reciting poems.

Other features of the Folk Festival may be folk dancing, Christmas songs of other lands, games and local carols, exchange of gifts around the Christmas tree, and refreshments.

Christmas Travelogue:

A carol may be dramatized, as "O Little Town of Bethlehem," "God Rest Ye Merry, Gentlemen," "Silent Night," etc. Another group may dramatize one or two foreign Christmas customs.

Mother Goose:

Instead of Santa Claus, Mother Goose may arrive with costumed characters, as "Snow White and the Seven Dwarfs," "Hansel and Gretel," or other characters desired. They distribute gifts, and may offer a brief program.

Mother Goose Party:

A party may be built around Mother Goose stories. Definite characterizations should be allotted before the party to each member. Each makes a brief dramatization of the character he or she represents. This may be done individually or in groups.

Christmas Story Book:

Construct a frame about six feet high and seven feet wide, and cover it with Christmas decorations. Dramatize the following: *(Tableau is recommended.)*

1—COVER DESIGN The manger scene.
2—CHRISTMAS CUSTOMS—*(See Christmas Folk Festival.)*
3—DICKEN'S CHRISTMAS CAROL—A section of the Carol read off stage and dramatized.
4—*Christmas Music*—A carol sung or dramatized.
5—*Christmas Toys*—Persons representing Christmas toys.
6—CHRISTMAS FASHIONS—A fashion review.
7—THE NIGHT BEFORE CHRISTMAS—A dramatization from the well-known poem by *Clement Moore*.

A Letter to Santa Claus:

Pass out paper and pencils after dividing the guests into equal groups. Instruct each group to compose a letter to Santa, using in sequence sentences beginning with the letters from the words "SANTA CLAUS."

A variation is to compose a letter from the word "CHRISTMAS."

Christmas Cut-Up Puzzle:

Have several well-known pictures relative to the season cut in pieces and deposited in boxes. Pass out the boxes to groups, supplying paste and a cardboard or paper upon which to paste the picture. The group assembling its picture correctly in the shortest time wins the game.

Santa's Shop:

An effective Christmas stunt is to represent Santa inspecting various dolls, male and female, in his toy shop. He should give a dialogue as he tests each doll to hear it cry, sing, or to watch it walk or perform in another manner. He presses a button on the chest or turns a crank at the side or on the back of each doll. After the inspection is complete, Santa is elated and has all of the dolls perform their individual mechanical functions in a drill before beginning his Christmas Eve journey. If this stunt is done in costumes and facial make-up to represent racial, antique and modern dolls, the stunt will be very colorful. All muscular movements should be mechanical.

CHAPTER TWO

Circle And Line Games

Bear in the Pit:

The players form a circle with interlocked hands. The bear, who is "IT," may push against the hands of the players and employ various ruses to get out of the circle. He is a very cunning fellow, but he is not rough in his play. Once he has escaped from the pit, by pretending to duck under one couple's arms but dashing out under another, or through any other cunning ruse, he is pursued by the other players. The person catching him becomes the bear.

Bird, Beast, or Fish:

"IT" stands before the seated players, and suddenly points his finger at some one and says, "Bird, (Beast), (or Fish)— One, two, three, four, five, six, seven, eight, nine, ten. The person to whom he pointed his finger must give the name of a bird, beast, or fish not mentioned in the game before. If the player is able to give the name before "IT" stops counting, then "IT" must endeavor to trap another individual. Players failing to answer correctly or happening to mention a name already given become "IT."

Blind Man:

Various obstacles, as: chairs, pails, and other items, are placed in a room into which the players are led. After the players have walked around or been led over these, they are taken to a room where they are blindfolded. Then they are told to work their way to the other end of the room in which the obstacles have been placed. While the blindfolds are being placed on the players an assistant of the game leader removes all of the objects from the center of the floor.

A variation may be to give each blindfolded player a cane, after he has been turned around several times, and to let him work his way to a spot indicated before he was blindfolded.

The temptation may be for an occasional reader to use this game as a means to obtain a hearty laugh at the expense of one or a few blindfolded players. The real purpose of play is not to laugh at but to laugh with other players. Unless this game is used as a group activity, in which the entire group may laugh and enjoy the game together, it should not be played.

Barnyard Chorus:

Groups are chosen to imitate the vocal sounds of various fowls and animals. At a given signal from the game leader the fowls and animals try to drown out each other with the individual group sounds.

The custom of selecting one player as a donkey, and to have him bray alone amid the laughter of the other players, is discouraged.

Blind Man's Bluff:

One player is blindfolded in the center of the circle. He is spun around several times, after which the circle moves and the blind man says, "Stop!" The circle stops and he endeavors to identify a player so as to make him the blind man. Scarfs, sweaters, hats, etc., may be exchanged by the players in an attempt to make identity more difficult. The blind man may run his hands over the hair, face or shoulders of a player. If his identity is correct, the person whom he identified becomes the blind man, the circle turns, and the game continues.

Animal Blind Man's Bluff:

This game is very popular among children and young people, and is played the same as the above game with the exception that identity is made by vocal sound;—the player imitating the grunt of a pig, the crow or a rooster, the mew of a cat, etc. The blind man tells the player what fowl or animal to imitate vocally. A favorite expression is, "Grunt, Piggy, grunt!" The person who is "IT" is not permitted to place his hands on a player.

Brother and Sister:

Two circles are formed with partners facing each other. At the first note of music, each circle begins moving in an opposite direction to the other until the music stops. Then each person must find his partner and reform the circle before the music starts.

This game may be played with penalties for those who fail to find a partner,—not necessarily the original partner,—or to be in position in the circle, before the music starts. Unsuccessful persons must drop from the game. The game may continue down to the last four people who circle around an object,—a table, group of chairs, etc. When the circles become small, barriers may be placed between marching partners as in Musical Chair.

Bull in the Pen:

This game is played the same as BEAR IN THE PIT with the exception that the bull may crash through the interlocked hands of the players by throwing all of his force against them.

While this game is enjoyed by boys, it is very rough and is not recommended for the averaged mixed party.

Buzz:

The players are seated in a circle or square. Beginning with the leader each player counts off consecutively, as "One," "Two," "Three," "Four," "Five," "Six," "Buzz." The numbers are raised as the game continues. Each seventh person must say, "Buzz" to a number beginning or ending with seven or any multiple of seven. The person failing to say, "Buzz" at the proper time must drop from the game. The game may continue down to the last two players.

For small children the game should be simplified so that a player would say, "Buzz" only to numbers ending with seven.

Caterpillar:

The players are seated in a circle with "IT" standing in the center. The players shift from chair to chair, in one direction, without arising to their feet, as they sing a song. The object is for the circle to keep in motion, each player to arrive on another chair, and for the person who is "IT" to obtain a chair which he or another player has crowded a person off. Chairs should be kept close together and the circle should always be as perfect as possible. Arm chairs are not used in this game.

Because this game is very rough it is not recommended for the average house party unless very rugged chairs are used.

Drop the Handkerchief:

This old game continues to be popular for out-of-door activities. A circle is formed with all of the players facing the center. The person who is "IT" runs on the outside of the circle with a handkerchief in his hand. He may employ various ruses, as pretending to drop the handkerchief behind one player but running on and dropping it behind another. When the handkerchief is dropped behind a player, that one gives chase to the runner. The object is for the runner to get to the vacant place in the circle before being tagged. If he is successful the pursuer becomes "IT" and the game continues. Otherwise the first runner continues to be "IT."

Follow the Leader:

While this game is popular for out-of-doors, it may be played in large rooms. The leader is at the head of the line. He may mount various obstacles, perform difficult tricks, make facial expressions, sing a comical song, or do anything humorous. All of the players follow his every movement until

they are led back to their original formation, until the pre-
announced final stunt has been performed, or announcement
of the conclusion is made.

A variation may be to have the group secretly select and then
announce to the pre-appointed leader a difficult stunt to perform. If he can not do it, the person next to him becomes
leader, and the leader goes to the rear of the line.

Fox and Geese:

On a large circle made on the earth or snow by a stick or
player's heel, about twenty-five to thirty feet in diameter, bases
are made at intersecting lines across the circle. These lines
form a hub in the center where stands the chaser who is
"IT." The players attempt to cross the intersecting lines without being caught. Neither runner nor chaser is permitted to
get off a line at any time. The only time a player is permitted
to run around the circle or on the circle line is when a base
next to him is vacant. The chaser is the Fox. The players are
the Geese. If the Fox catches a player he becomes the Fox
and the Fox becomes a Goose.

Fruit Basket:

Arrange equal numbers of chairs in two opposite rows facing each other across the room, or at least fifteen feet apart.
All chairs are occupied. One or two persons stand between
the rows, depending upon the size of the group. Each line
leader names his team persons after some fruit or vegetable.
"IT" calls at least two fruits or vegetables at a time, or a fruit
and a vegetable, depending upon the rules of the game. Such
persons called must arise and exchange chairs. "IT" tries to
obtain a vacant chair. If he is successful the person left standing must be "IT."

Sometimes the game is played by "IT" occasionally crying,
"Fruit Basket Upset!" or "Change!" In that event all players
must race across the room for a seat in the other line. The
person left standing becomes "IT."

Grand March:

FIRST, the players are arranged in couples so as to form a double file, boys in one line, girls in the other. A leader is at the head of each line. At the beginning of the music the double file moves to the rear center of the room, comes down the middle of the floor to the front center, where one line turns right, the other turns left.

SECOND, upon reaching the rear corners of the room, each leader makes a sharp turn toward the center, so that the lines intersect at a forty-five degree angle,—each person passing in turn through the opposite line, forming the figure "X."

THIRD, the lines are brought together into a double file, coming down the middle of the floor to the end of the room, where one couple turns right, the next turns left, meeting at the opposite end in flank formation of *fours,* forming a revolving wagon wheel in the center of the floor.

FOURTH, from the wagon-wheel formation, the procession of *fours* continue to the end of the room, where, again, one couple turns right, the other left. At the opposite end of the room single files are formed, coming into separate winding spools around each leader. The music stops as the winding is completed. The music is continued and the unwinding is accomplished with the end person in each line leading his file. The music stops. A right-about-face is made. The music continues, double and flank formation of *fours* are executed, coming to the center of the room where a fan formation is made.

FIFTH, the procession is brought back to single lines and then formed into separate double files, boys in one, girls in the other, with both files meeting at the end center, as in No. 3. Instead of each couple turning right and left, the boys separate, face each other, raise both hands to form an arch for the girls to pass through. Each pair of boys, after passing through the arch, separate to form an arch.

The girls break into single files and come down each side of the room, meeting at end center to form arches for the boys to pass through. The boys pass through the girls' arch in double file.

SIXTH, the original couples are brought into double file. Then, at the room end, center, the girls step in front of each male partner, forming one single line. This line continues marching around the room, either straight or zig-zag, until all have been brought into single formation. Then the leading girl leads the line to the center of the room, where she begins to revolve, each person following her until the entire line is wound into one large revolving spool. Here the game may end, or when the boys and girls are brought back into partner formation. (See No. 4.)

This game is designed as a "mixer," to prevent the shy from being isolated or one individual being with another the entire evening. Another "Getting Acquainted" game may be used after or following this game to help the group exchange partners.

In small spaces the Grand March may be simplified by using only the single and double file formation.

Hot Potato:

*The group is formed into a circle or square and is given an unbreakable object to pass from hand to hand during music or between the leader's whistle blasts: a newspaper, handkerchief, ball, piece of wood, etc. The person holding the object when the signal to stop passing has been given is eliminated.

In large groups those who drop the object may also be eliminated.

Jacob and Rachel:

A circle is formed, players holding hands. Jacob and Rachel are on the inside. Jacob is blindfolded. He asks, "Rachel, where are thou?" As she endeavors to evade him, by ducking under his arms, past him, or on tip-toe just behind him, she replies in a quality of voice she chooses, "Here I am, Jacob." Each time he asks the question she must answer. If he catches her, a new Jacob is chosen. She may become Jacob, or a different boy and girl may be selected for the parts.

Leap Frog:

The players are formed in a single line. Each person, except the end player, bends with his back horizontal and palms flat on the ground. The end player begins leaping over the others until he reaches the head of the line, where he takes the position of the other players. Then the next end player leaps over his mates and bends into his former position at the head of the line. Each end player does likewise until all of the players have participated.

This is a very popular game for boys, but it should not be continued too long.

The Junk Man:

A circle is formed by the players with the Junk Man, who is "IT," being in the center. Pretending he has a bag of junk on his shoulder, he approaches a player by stomping on the floor. The person before whom he stands says, "Who's there?" He answers, "The Junk Man. . . . Have you any old rags, paper, iron or rubber today?" The player replies, "No, but you may find some at the .... house to your ....
(Number   (Direction)
on this street." *(The player must mention the third to the sixth house to the Right or to the Left,—meaning the third to sixth player to the Right or Left.)*

The person indicated must begin to run on the outside of the circle in the direction given. The Junk Man must begin the pursuit. Should either he or the person in the circle move in the wrong direction, both are penalized. He must go to the center of the circle, the Junk Pile, and remain inactive there during the game. The person in the circle becomes "IT," and the circle closes the vacated position.

While neither the runner nor the Junk Man *dare* cut through the circle, the Junk Man may run on the inside and cut to the outside at any point while he does run across the circle. Once a runner has arrived at his vacated position in the circle, he may continue by running on the inside and standing before another player, forcing that player to be pursued. Should the Junk Man fail to catch the second player he must go to the junk pile, and the runner becomes the Junk Man. **Any** player who is tagged before arriving at his vacated position in the circle must go to the Junk Pile. The game continues until the Junk Pile becomes so large that movement on the inside of the circle is impossible.

Musical Chair:

Arrange a line of chairs with every other one reversed so that one player, when seated, will face in one direction and the next player in the opposite direction. Appoint a leader to begin the procession around the chairs, and have one more player than chairs. When the music is in process the players march. When it stops they sit down, and one chair is taken from the line for each person excluded. The person not obtaining a chair is eliminated. The last person seated, among the last two players marching, has the game. During the marching hands should be kept from the chairs. For large groups, two or more players may be eliminated each time the music stops.

Neighbors:

"IT" stands in the center of the circle or square, quickly pointing his finger at a player and saying either, "Right," or "Left," as he rapidly counts from one to ten. The person to whom he points is supposed to tell the given and surname of the person to his right or left, depending upon what "IT" asked him. A player who fails to respond or is in error becomes "IT."

Nuts:

The players are seated in two opposite lines, the same as in Fruit Basket, and are given the names of various nuts. The game is played as is Fruit Basket.

Partner Tag:

Partners with arms locked stand either in a circle or a line. One person is the runner. Another is the chaser. If the game is being played "in line," the line may weave in and out to obstruct the progress of the chaser, and to help the runner, "IT," from being tagged. The runner may hook arms with another couple at any time, forcing the third person of that group to be "IT." Should the chaser tag the runner, the runner must pursue the chaser. To keep interest high, as many runners as possible should be released during a game.

Instead of the game being played in line formation, couples may stand anywhere within a room, permitting only enough space for the runners to get through. Much fun is had if the chaser is compelled to follow the course of the runner between the standing couples.

Poor Pussy:

The players are seated in a circle with Pussy in the center. Pussy moves to any individual, kneels and begins to meow. The player must stroke Pussy's head three times and say, "Poor Pussy, Poor Pussy, Poor Pussy," without smiling. Any player who smiles while Pussy is kneeling or acting before him must take Pussy's place. Pussy may create humorous situations in an endeavor to make the players laugh.

Red Riding Hood:

The player, who is the Wolf, has a dust cap or handkerchief over his head, walking on the outside of the circle, touching another player on the back and saying gruffly: "I'm the Big, Bad Wolf." The player replies, "Why, Grandma, what large eyes you have!" The wolf retorts, "I'm not your grandma." The question is asked, "Oh, you're not? Whose grandma are you?" The wolf then describes a player's hair, facial features and clothing. As soon as the player recognizes it is he whom the wolf is after, he begins running from him. If he is tagged before regaining his place in the circle, he is "IT." The Wolf should not describe a player so close to him that he has the advantage of catching him.

Folk Lore Games:

The young and old appreciate folk tales. Mother Goose and other stories present possibilities to the game leader or householder who might desire to build an original game by adapting a story to an old pattern. The preceding game is given as an example.

Revolving Circles:

The players are formed in two circles, an inner and an outer; one of boys and one of girls. While the music is being played the circles revolve in opposite directions. When it stops, each boy and girl opposite each other must introduce themselves by exchanging their names, interlocking arms, and dancing in a circle until they are in their original formation. The music may be resumed at any time. Interest is increased by causing the dancing partners to rush for their positions in the revolving circles.

This may be made an elimination game by penalizing all persons who fail to be in position when the music starts.

Ring on A String:

The group is seated in a circle having a continuous cord string upon which a ring has been threaded. The ring is passed from hand to hand of the players by an in and out motion of the hands during the singing of a familiar song. The object is to keep the ring passing from one player to the other without the person who is "IT" observing in whose hand it is. "IT" may ask any player to open one or both hands at any time. The players must comply. The person in whose hand the ring is found becomes "IT." The players may employ various ruses to fool "IT," as pretending to refuse acceptance or being anxious to pass it on.

Store:

A person who is appointed "IT" leaves the room. Then the group decides upon what kind of a store to represent: grocery, hardware, shoe, fruit, etc. As soon as the type is agreed upon and items from the store have been allotted each player, "IT" is called into the room. Upon his entry he is asked whether he wants it shouted or whispered. He makes his selection, where upon the group replies by shouting or whispering each allotted item simultaneously. "IT" may ask the group to repeat, either in whispering or shouting, as many times as he desires. If he recognizes the store another person becomes "IT" and the game continues, or "IT" may wish to return to the room where he was in seclusion while the group selects another store.

Spin the Platter:

This game may be played traditionally or according to the revised method listed below.

Traditional Method:

The players are seated in circle or square and numbered consecutively, girls with even numbers and boys with odd. "IT," who is in the center of the circle or square, spins the plate or platter, calling out a number of the opposite sex. The person having that number must rush to catch the spinning object before it comes to rest on the floor. Failure to do so before the object stops spinning makes the unsuccessful person "IT."

A variation is to call names instead of numbers of the opposite sex. This method, however, has proved unsuccessful because of the tendency of some individuals to pay more attention to one or two persons. Numbers makes it somewhat more difficult to pick out definite persons, if the game is not prolonged.

Revised Method:

The above formation and numbers are used. The difference is that all chairs must be occupied so as to have one more person than chairs. "IT" may cry at any time, "Break the plate!"

whereupon each player must rush across the circle for another chair. The person failing to obtain a seat becomes "IT."

This method is very rough but popular wherever it has been tried. Provision for a new platter is occasionally necessary where a group plays the game often.

Stage Coach:

The players are seated in a circle or square. One person is chosen as the Narrator to begin the game. Each player is silently given a part of the stage coach, including passengers and their baggage, driver, and his accessories, and horses with their harness.

When all persons have been given parts in a whisper by the leader, the Narrator begins his story, making it up as he progresses, and mentioning various parts of coach, etc. Each time he mentions a part or passenger, etc., related to a player, that player arises, turns around in a complete circle and sits down. At any time he says, "Stage Coach," all players must arise and turn around and sit down. If at any time the coach upsets or meets with disaster, all must arise and rush for another seat. The person failing to obtain a chair becomes the Narrator and the story continues.

Three Deep:

A double circle is formed, all persons facing the center of the circle. The game begins with a Chaser and a 'Runner on the outside of the circle. The Chaser pursues the Runner. The Runner at any time may run to the inside of the circle and stand in front of a couple, thus making the circle at that point three deep. Immediately the person on the outside of the circle becomes the one pursued. Should the Runner be tagged by the Chaser at any time he becomes the Chaser and the Chaser becomes the Runner. To keep interest high, the runner should run around the circle once before stopping in front of a couple.

Ventriloquist:

The players are formed in a circle with the Ventriloquist, who is "IT," operating on the outside of the circle. Each person is given a terse sentence to repeat when approached by the Ventriloquist, and another terse sentence or word which is common to the entire circle but unknown by the Ventriloquist.

The Ventriloquist's usual method for causing his "dummies" to talk is to place his hand on their backs. He may employ various ruses to have as many dummies talking as possible, by placing his hand on the back of one person but rushing to another to have him perform. The player is to perform any reasonable stunt requested. The Ventriloquist may move the head, arm or entire body of a player. All movements should be mechanical. But he can not pause behind one player before going to another. Should he use the forbidden sentence or word, he is chased, and the person catching him becomes the Ventriloquist. Then the circle is reformed, the secret sentence or word is changed, and the game is continued.

Wink:

A circle is formed with girls seated, boys standing behind each chair, and one more chair than girls. The boy behind the vacant chair winks at a girl who tries to get to his chair before the boy behind her tags her. Should she flee from the boy behind her, that boy must wink at one or more girls until his chair is occupied. No girl is permitted to leave a chair immediately after being tagged by the boy behind her.

CHAPTER THREE

Relays and Races

Apple Relay—(The Bender):

The group is equally divided into two teams with a captain each. A chalk toe line for each team is established near the end of the room, and a half-bushel basket for each team is placed six feet from the toe line toward the wall. Each team is provided with two one-quart fruit baskets and two apples. Each team is in single file with the person at the head of the line standing at the toe line. Each captain is at the rear of the line with the baskets and apples at his feet.

At the starting signal the captain passes to the player ahead of him an empty fruit basket over the player's right shoulder. The player receives it and places it on the floor at his right foot. Next, the captain passes an apple over the player's left shoulder. The player places the apple in the basket. Then the captain passes the second basket over the player's right shoulder. The player places that at his left foot. Lastly, the captain passes the second apple over the player's left shoulder. The player places that in the remaining empty basket. After this operation has been completed, the player passes the baskets and the apples to the person ahead of him as he received each article beginning with the first item received—an empty basket, then an apple, etc. This process continues until the baskets and apples have been received by the person at the head of the line. He takes the apples, one at a time, and throws them into the half-bushel basket, after which he reclaims them, picks up the quart baskets and rushes to the rear of the line. He passes the baskets and apples to the captain as they were previously passed. The game concludes after the captain has thrown the apples at the toe line. The team finishing first wins the game.

Artistic Pictures:

Divide the players into small groups. Give each group a drawing pencil, charcoal or crayons, and a piece of paper for each member. Each person of the group draws a member's picture, in turn. The group having the best pictures wins a prize. Some of the results will be very amusing.

Art Modeling:

Divide the players into *fours* or *fives*, and give each group a card table and an equal amount of modeling clay. Each group then decides upon some person or object to model. The group presenting the best model at the conclusion of the appointed time wins a prize.

An equal number of toothpicks should be given each group as an aid to reproducing people, the toothpicks being used for legs and arms.

Chewing Gum Modeling:

When chewing gum is used instead of modeling clay, each person is given one to two sticks to chew and a small piece of cardboard upon which to work. More toothpicks should be given than with the clay contest so as to handle the chewing gum.

Apple Race,—Nosey:

A central goal line and opposite team starting lines are established by chalk marks on the floor. Two teams with a captain each are formed, and an apple for each participating team mate is placed on each starting line. At a given signal, the game begins by each person pushing his apple to the goal line with his nose. The team having all of its apples over the goal line in the shortest time wins the race.

This race may be conducted by using marbles, rubber balls, dried peas, etc.

Bag Race:

Determine a starting and a finishing line, about seventy-five feet apart. To each contestant give a burlap bag in which he places his feet and holds the top with his hands. Place each player on the starting line. At the given signal each person begins hopping toward the finishing line. The person arriving first wins the race.

Out-Door Balloon Race:

Give each contestant a deflated balloon to blow up as large as possible in a set time.

In-Door Balloon Race:

Deflated balloons are blown as large as possible, after the starting signal is given. At the second blast of the whistle, each player balances his balloon on a tea spoon or table knife, which has been given him by the game leader, and begins carrying his balloon to the finishing line. If he drops the balloon he must start over. The first person to reach the finishing line wins.

Balloon Relay:

The members of each team blow up a balloon, except the guards at the goal line. At the second whistle blast, each person with a balloon begins blowing his toward the goal line, where the guards or an equal number of team mates begin blowing the balloons back to the finishing line. The team having the greatest number of balloons over the finishing line in the appointed time wins. Balloons are suspended in the air only by players blowing against them. Any player who permits his balloon to fall to the floor must kneel on his knees, raise the balloon with his hands and begin suspending it with his breath before he arises to his feet.

Clothesline Race:

Select two teams, each with a captain. Stretch two clotheslines, one for each team, equi-distant from each team's starting point or goal line. Give each team a clothes hamper filled with an equal number of male and female attire, and an equal number of clothespins. At the starting signal each captain takes the team hamper from the starting line and hangs each garment, racing back to his waiting team mate with the empty hamper. That player takes the hamper, races to the clothes-lines, takes down each garment, folding each, and placing each in the hamper. Then he races back to the next waiting team mate who rushes to the line and rehangs each garment. This activity continues until all of the team have participated.

Clothespin Relay:

Upon two equally distant lines place an equal number of clothespins, after two teams, each with a captain have been drawn. Each team has a basket or clothespin bag. At the starting signal the first member of each team races from the team line with the basket or bag to pick up the clothespins. Then he rushes back to the line, gives the filled container to the waiting player, who hastens to relay the clothespins. The laying and picking up of the clothespins continues until the captain is at the head of the line again.

Variation: Two teams in file formation face each other, each passing twelve clothespins singly down the line overhand; each player grasping his neighbor's right wrist with his left hand, and passing with his free hand. All clothespins dropped must be picked up without breaking the line or an individual grasp of another player's wrist.

Pick-up and Lay-down Relays:

By using the methods described in the preceding relays;— selecting two teams with a captain for each, and having each team in single file on opposite sides of the room—other objects may be used, as: Marbles, small rubber balls, dried peas or beans, corn, unshelled peanuts, and other objects, for "pick-up," and "lay-down" relays.

*¹ Doughnut Race:

Stretch a line and tie doughnuts to it. Cord strings with doughnuts attached should be tied to the taut line and dropped so as to be in line with the contestants' mouths. Blindfold each player and stand them before a doughnut. Hands may be tied behind the back. The person who eats all of his doughnut first wins.

*¹ Eating Races and Relays:

The reader may build various "eating" races and relays by, first, following the above method; second, by having one partner feed another; or third, by blindfolding each and having both seated not too close to each other, with one feeding and the other eating. Apples, marshmallows, unshelled peanuts, cake, pie, gruel and cereals, bottled beverages, etc., may be used. Aprons or bibs should be provided for the "eaters," when there is the possibility of soiling the clothing.

Spearing:

Eating races and relays may be conducted with the use of cooked vegetables by seating the contestants at a table, providing an equal amount of whole peas, beans, or diced fruit or vegetables to be speared or taken to the mouth with either one or two toothpicks. When two toothpicks are used they serve as chop sticks.

Feather Race:

Each player is placed on a previously established starting line, and is given a *down* feather (a light, fluffy feather from a common fowl). At the starting signal, every one tosses his

---

*¹ Footnote:

Precaution should be taken that no food such as crackers, or other dry edibles should be used in eating races or relays, because of the danger of choking.

feather into the air and begins blowing it to the finishing line. The person getting his feather over the finishing line first wins the race. After the feather is once suspended, no player is permitted to touch it unless it falls to the floor. Then he is permitted to pick it up and upon his knees begin to blow it again into the air.

Feather Relay:

A feather relay may be built by combining the above game with the instructions for a Balloon Relay. (See page 49.)

Handkerchief Race:

With the contestants on the starting line, and a handkerchief apiece being at their feet, at the starting signal each player stoops, picks up the handkerchief with his teeth and races toward the finishing line.

Handkerchief Relay:

By using relay rules the Handkerchief Race may be converted into a relay.

Knife and Spoon Races and Relays:

By following either race or relay rules, competitive events may be made by suspending or picking up and carrying objects from a starting point to a goal with either a knife or spoon. Penalties may be imposed for dropping articles, touching another article in the line with the working tool, or failing to drop the article in the receptacle at the goal line. Suggested articles to carry are: dried peas or beans, corn or other dried grain, whole or shelled peanuts and small green apples, also marbles and large round beads. When using a perfectly round object a spoon should be used instead of a knife. To pick up such an object without touching it with one's fingers or hand is almost impossible, but affords much fun. No player should be permitted to get an object against anything to pick it up, or to suspend it on a knife or spoon. Tea spoons should be used.

Marble Relay:

Provide each team with an equal number of marbles, a tea spoon and a quart fruit basket. The teams are lined in a single file. The captain lays the marbles, which are in the basket, upon small paper bases laid in line along one side of the room, and are equal distances apart. (Each team has a row of bases.) As soon as he has all bases filled he rushes back to his waiting team mate with the empty basket, then to the rear of the line. The next person at the head of the line begins picking up the marbles and placing them in the basket. Picking up and laying down the marbles continue until the captain is again at the head of the line.

Marble Tossing Relay:

A team toe line is established. A quart fruit basket is placed six feet beyond the line. The players are arranged in single file, the first man at the toe line. In turn, each member of each team tries to toss an equal number of marbles into the basket. No person is permitted to step or bend over the toe line, but must stand erect. As soon as an individual has tossed the marbles he retrieves them, hands them to the next player, and rushes to the rear of the line. Each marble remaining in the basket counts one point for the team. Each marble bouncing out or thrown outside of the basket causes a loss of one point.

_____

This activity may be carried by the use of small green fruit, unripe apples, plums, peaches, etc. This is very difficult.

Pig Race:

A finishing line is marked about fifty feet from the starting line. The contestants are paired off, one acting as the pig, the other as the rider. The pig runs on all "fours" to the finishing line. The other person rides on his back. The rider need not sit erect. Any position by which he can hold on is permitted.

The distance for the race should not exceed sixty to seventy-five feet.

As an out-door or gymnasium race this game affords much fun.

The Bull's Eye:

Tossing races and relays may be executed by making a bull's eye of large cardboard and standing it on edge. A round hole, three to four inches in diameter, should be cut in the center of the cardboard. The board should be rigid and braced against two chairs or on an easel. Marbles or small rubber balls are recommended for tossing through the bull's eye.

Three-Leg Race:

A starting and a finishing line having been established, the contestants are grouped in pairs, with the right leg of one and the left leg of the other tied together with a handkerchief or scarf. The contestants are placed on the starting line. At the whistle blast or starting signal, all race toward the finishing line. The pair arriving first wins the game. Rope or twine should not be used to bind the legs. The danger involved is too great.

Tug of War:

Two teams are chosen, each placed at the end of a heavy rope which has been marked with a handkerchief or cloth tied around the center. A central goal line is marked on the ground. The center of the rope is suspended above this line at the beginning of the contest. The object is for one team to pull the other across the goal line. Teams should be numerically equal, and closely divided in strength.

Wheelbarrow Race:

The contestants are divided in pairs, one person to run on his hands and being pushed by his team mate who holds his feet as the "handle bars." Each person acting as the wheelbarrow has his hands on the starting line. At the starting signal each pair, the wheelbarrow and the pusher, labor toward the finishing line. The pair arriving first wins the game.

CHAPTER FOUR

Miscellaneous Contests

Conducting Contests:

The author suggests grouping the players into teams of five to ten people in the average contest, giving a card or slip of paper and a pencil to each team. This system eliminates individual competition and provides for more wholesome fun and play.*

Advertisements:

Advertisement contests have been listed elsewhere. Repetition is here made to indicate the possibilities for other games by using advertisements.

1. Cut advertisements from magazines and hang them about the room. Number each. Names and trade marks should be eliminated or covered. Provide papers and pencils for the players and have them identify the advertisements consecutively. The person or group with the highest score wins.

2. An auto race, radio, electrical appliance, food or style display may be made and named according to desire by cutting out special advertisements and having the contestants classify each by the manufacture or trade name.

3. Travelogues, authors, famous persons, wonders of the world, shrines, people of the community, and other games may be played by using nameless advertisements or pictures. Example: "PEOPLE OF OUR VILLAGE,"—FRED CANFIELD;—The letter "F" before the word "RED" or a section of red paper. Following this is an advertisement or picture of a can, and another of a field.

Alphabet:

Supply the teams with large cardboard letters, enough to form common words. One team secretly selects a word to spell. Letters to form the word are individually allotted to the various team members by the captain, and each person rushes to the pre-established team goal line, holding the letters above their heads. The other team or teams are supposed to recognize and call out the word before it is formed. A team recognizing an unformed word wins one point. Any team failing to complete the word before an opponent calls it loses one point. The team with the highest score wins.

Variation:

A variation may be for each team to have their letters jumbled on a table. The game leader calls a word. The team being able to spell out the word at its goal line with the single letters in the shortest time scores one point. Others sustain an equal loss.

Authors:

Provide paper and pencils. Upon the slips of paper, the following or similar statements have been written in advance:

1. The name of a pullet's coop, and he might have qualified for a Tall Man's Club.

Answer: *Henry Longfellow.*

2. Winsome the name that ends with ton, when by the kirk on a hill.

Answer: *Winston Churchill.*

3. He wrote in Old England with a will and an "I am," and the end of his name was like a quaking arrow.

Answer: *William Shakespeare.*

4. His first name was the same as that of an Apostle, his second was funny and more, and he lived in the time of hand-made barrels.

Answer: *James Fenimore Cooper.*

5. He was famous for a special huckleberry and he might have been called the "Two."

Answer: *Mark Twain.*

6. John said, "In the winter this leaf is green," with wit and then a "titter."
Answer: *John Greenleaf . Whittier.*
7. "Jack, you win," said the miller.
Answer: *Joaquin Miller.*
8. A ruddy face, a pretty yard; a skip and then a fling.
Answer: *Rudyard Kipling.*
9. The robber told Bert to dress his burns.
Answer: *Robert Burns.*
10. "Phil, gather cowslips by the brooks."
Answer: *Phillips Brooks.*

The players are to give the answers. The person or team with the highest score wins the game. With a little thought the game leader may build various games on this pattern, extending to radio and movie stars, people of the community, etc.

Dumb Crambo:

The guests are divided into two groups: first, the audience which is seated in the room; second, those who retire to another room while the audience selects a word to be acted. When the word has been selected the second group, or "actors," enter. The word is described to them, they try to act it. If they guessed wrong, the audience may "boo" or clap their hands in disapproval. Three chances are given the "actors" to guess and act the word correctly. If they can not guess the first word another is selected. When a word has been guessed and acted correctly the actors become the audience and the audience becomes the actors. The group wins which guesses and acts out the word correctly in the shortest time.

Gossip:

The players are formed in a circle or square. The leader begins the game by whispering a statement very rapidly in the ear of the person sitting next to him. The statement, or assumed words, are passed on by the same method from person to person until the last player. He is to tell what he thought was whispered in his ear. Then the leader tells what he actually told the first person.

Moon Is Round:

The leader begins the game by holding a pointer or cane or yardstick in his left hand and saying, "The moon is round. It has eyes, nose and a mouth." While giving the dialogue the person is to begin by drawing an imaginary circle on the floor and then to indicate eyes, nose and mouth. Much fun is had by others trying the same thing but not holding the indicator in the left hand.

Musical Love Story:

The pianist is informed what songs to play in advance. The leader reads the statements after which the pianist plays a small portion of the song—merely enough to catch the theme. The players write the answers on provided slips of paper.

1. A young man met a maiden. He did not know her name until she sang . . .
Answer: *Sweet Genevieve.*

Her name was not sufficient. He asked her where he might meet her. She replied . . .
Answer: *In the Gloaming.*

3. That evening as he tried to embrace her he said, with a sigh . . .
Answer: *When You Come to the End of A Perfect Day.*

4. He saw her the next morning and said . . .
Answer: *Howdy.*

5. She expressed her sentiments with . . .
Answer: *Smiles.*

6. She thought they were making wonderful headway, as he whispered in her ear . . .
Answer: *Dear Old Pal of Mine.*

7. They were quietly married . . .
Answer: *After the Ball.*

8. They honeymooned under . . .
Answer: *Carolina Moon.*

9. They started home . . .
Answer: *Comin' Thro' the Rye.*

10. Five years later the neighbors said . . .
Answer: *John Brown Has A Little Injun.*

Name Me:

This activity affords much fun as a getting acquainted game. Pin the name of an animal, tree, or flower on the back of each guest. Each person tries to learn from other players what he is, as he asks various questions and they make ambiguous replies. Each question should be answered relative to the description of the animal, tree, or flower, but not so as to make identity easy. Three questions may be asked by each person. If unsuccessful they must part and endeavor to learn their identities from other players. The first ten players to identify themselves correctly receive a bag of popcorn to share equally.

Name Them:

Each player is provided with paper and pencil and is instructed to secure as many autographs as possible in the designated time. The game begins at the starting signal. The person having the most autographs wins.

Observation:

Prepare various objects on a tray or tea table in advance of the party. Uncover the arrangement, permitting the players to observe the articles for a brief period. Then pass out paper and pencils and have each note the articles. The person with the highest score wins.

Penny Contest:

Provide each player or team with a Lincoln Penny, paper and pencil. Instruct each person to write numerically the answers to the following:

1. Find a fruit.
Answer: *Date*.
2. Find flowers.
Answer: *Two lips (tulips)*.
3. Find a bridge.
Answer: *Bridge of nose*.

4. Find an animal.
Answer: *Hare (hare)*.

5. Find part of a hill.
Answer: *The brow*.

6. Find part of a corn stalk.
Answer: *Ear*.

7. Find part of a railroad track.
Answer: *Tie*.

8. Find a messenger.
Answer: *One Sent (one cent)*.

9. Find a country.
Answer: *United States of America*.

10. Find a motto.
Answer: *In God We Trust*.

11. Find what all people love.
Answer: *Liberty*.

12. Find a weapon of punishment.
Answer: *The lash*.

13. The common word of an egotist.
Answer: *"I" (eye)*.

14. The part of an automobile spring.
Answer: *Leaves*.

15. Find something belonging to every animal.
Answer: *A coat*.

16. Find a part of a man's pipe.
Answer: *A stem*.

17. Find part of an automobile tire.
Answer: *The rim*.

18. Find something peculiar to a lion.
Answer: *A beard*.

19. Find something all dogs should have.
Answer: *A collar*.

20. What is possessed by meddlesome people?
Answer: *Cheek*.

Note: Have you ever tried this game with other coins? Study a dime or quarter and make up your own questions and answers. But be sure each player has an identical coin.

Babes in the Woods:

The players are formed into groups of "fours" with a fifth person in the center. The two extra persons as in *Rabbits* are Bad Wolves who bark after their prey and eliminate each person caught, by placing that person in an imaginary den in a corner of the room. If a wolf is tagged by the pursuing babes before reaching his den with a captured babe, he is eliminated. The game continues down to the last three groups. When the babes start pursuing the wolves, both must reach their den before being tagged. Upon the capture of four babes the group of "four" whose babe was captured first dissolves and become babes.

Cluck:

Groups of "fours," representing chicken coops, stand about the room having within, as in *Rabbits,* a fifth person who is a chick. The two extra persons are old hens, who cry, "Cluck, cluck," as they endeavor to tag a chick running from one coop to another. Two chicks dare not be in one coop at a time. A tagged chick becomes "IT" and a hen reverts to a chick.

Out-of-door Treasure Hunt:

The method for this game varies in that it requires larger objects, as old chairs, etc., which may be hidden in a half-mile radius of the place of meeting, and many require an hour or more to complete the hunt. A specific list of articles hidden should be read before the hunt begins.

Poet's Corner:

Select ten well-known poem titles. List them numerically on a slip of paper. Pass out paper and pencils and have the players write the name of the author as the title is read.

A variation is to select short passages from famous poems and read them, asking the players to write according to your decision the title or the author.

Proverbs:

Provide the players with paper and pencils. Quote familiar proverbs and have the contestants supply the part not quoted.

QUOTE   ANSWER

Example: 1—"A stitch in time ....*saves nine"*

Example: 2—"Beard the lion ....*in his den"*

Rats:

Formations are the same as in *Cluck,* and the playing principles are the same with the exception that instead of having two extra persons there are two extra groups who run in open circle formation after each rat running from one hole to another, and endeavor to trap him by getting him within the circle and enclosing him with interlocked hands, and eliminating him thereafter from the game. Each group of "fours" dissolve in succession, as in *Babes in the Woods,* and become rats. The last rat caught has the game. (*This game is recommended only for large groups playing in large spaces.*)

Scram:

Seat the women in a circle, each next to a vacant chair. The men, in an adjoining room, decide certain objects or the matter to discuss individually with the women. Then the men occupy the vacant chairs, begin their conversation with their respective women partners, endeavoring to obscure the subject they are talking about. The subjects may be either simple or difficult, as a certain chair or the vacuum in a light bulb in the room. When the woman identifies the subject, she says, "Scram!" whereupon the man moves to the next vacant chair. The men may move after asking three questions or at the signal of the leader's whistle. The woman who identifies the greatest number of subjects wins.

Scissors Crossed:

A pair of scissors are started crossed among the seated players. The object is to baffle the "unacquainted players with the trick involved. He who understands the game will pass the scissors either crossed or uncrossed by either crossing or un-crossing his legs at the time of passing. The person who un-derstands the trick will receive the scissors as they were passed. Example: One with his feet crossed passed the scissors crossed. Because he crossed his feet, he says, "Scissors crossed," and the one who receives them will immediately cross his feet and say, "Scissors crossed." Scissors uncrossed are the same, by persons having their feet uncrossed when passing.

Sewing Bee:

A very amusing pastime is to give each man one or a pair of socks to darn, and the woman an assignment, as a doll dress to make. A definite time limit is set. The persons with the greatest originality and workmanship win the game. For the doll dresses, patches from an apron or dress factory are recom-mended, because of their inexpensiveness.

Spelling Bee:

This old pastime is still very popular. Line the players in two files facing each other. Give each person a word to spell by rotating across the room from number one to number one, number two to number two, etc., until each person in each line has spelled or been eliminated by mis-spelling his word. The contest may continue down to the last two standing per-sons. The one standing longest wins the game.

States:

Give the players paper and pencil and tell them to write down ten nearby states. While practically all will begin writing down States of the United States of America, the cor-rect states are:
1. The state of Anxiety.
2. The state of Adversity.
3. The state of Being.
4. The state of Bliss.
5. The state of Boredom.

6. The state of Depression.
7. The state of Discouragement.
8. The state of Intoxication.
9. The state of Matrimony.
10. The state of Mind.

Suggestions for Building Contests:

Many games, because they are built on a common foundation, are very elastic and lend themselves to other suggestions. This is especially true of many paper and pencil games. The reader is advised to study the games herein for original possibilities. Suggestions for building one's own contests are:

1. Book Review, by listing popular book titles and asking the players to give the authors.

2. Birthday of Presidents, by listing the names and asking the dates.

3. Birthplaces of the Presidents and other Presidential games.

4. List suggestive prefixes or suffixes from your dictionary, such as in the game of the Witch's cats. Many possibilities are herein provided.

5. Capitols of States.
6. Famous Generals of a war.
7. Outstanding men of the present administration.
8. Famous Shrines.
9. Popular Songs.
10. Famous Quotations.
11. Local History.
12. Natural Wonders.
13. Early or Recent Inventions.
14. Principal Rivers.
15. Outstanding American Women, etc.

String Winding Contest:

Equally divide the guests into groups. Give each group a wound string or cord. At the starting signal, the captain of each group begins unwinding the string, while counting ten. At the arrival of "ten" he passes the ball on to the next person, and the process continues until the ball is completely unwound. Then the group begins to individually wind the string back into a ball by each person counting one to ten, as in the unwinding. The group completing first without winding snarls or knots into the ball wins the game. This game may be adapted to a race or relay.

Tagging the Mule:

Draw a mule on a large piece of paper, the mule being about two feet high. On a piece of bristol board or heavy paper draw the mule's tail. Cut this out for pinning on the first section. The players are blindfolded several feet from the suspended drawing and are told to pin the tail in the correct place on the mule. Much fun results from the various positions in which the tail is placed.

Tongue Twisting Contest:

Much fun may be had by having the players read a tongue twister from slips of paper upon which one has been written and passed to each individual to read consecutively.

Dewdrop:

"How much dew would a dewdrop drop if a dewdrop could drop dew?"

Peter Piper:

"Peter Piper picked a peck of pickle peppers; a peck of pickle peppers Peter Piper picked. If Peter Piper picked a peck of pickle peppers, where's the peck of pickle peppers Peter Piper picked?"

Sam Swan's Swan:

Sam Swan's swan swam with a swan's swan that swam with a swan's swan past Sam Swan's swan's swan. Said Sam Swan's swan to the swan's swan with the swan's swan, "Swim with the big swan's swan till my swan swims like a swan's swan past the swan's swan." So the swan swam to the swan, and Sam Swan's swan's swan was taught to swim until he and the swan's swan swam as rapidly as the swan and the swan's swan that passed Sam Swan's swan's swan. Thereafter Sam Swan's swan's swan skimmed the water as beautifully as the swan with a swan that swam with a swan's swan, and no more did Sam Swan's swan's swan lag behind the swan's swan that swam with a swan's swan.

Woodchuck:

"How much wood would a woodchuck chuck if a wood-chuck could chuck wood? He would chuck as much wood as woodchuck chucked if a woodchuck could chuck wood."

Do you recall other tongue twisters? For others, consult game books in the city library. Better still, try your luck at making one of your own, as the author did with "Sam Swan's Swan."

Treasure Hunt—(In-door):

Hide small objects about the room or rooms for the players to find. The person or group obtaining the most objects wins the game.

CHAPTER FIVE

Tricks and Mystery Games

These games have been taken from the book, "GAMES For QUIET HOURS And SMALL SPACES," National Recreation Association, New York City, and are used by Special Permission of that Association.

As a well known saying runs—"It's fun to be fooled but it's more fun to know." Tricks and mystery stunts are entertaining to watch, but it is more fun to perform them yourself. The tricks which follow are simple to master. They are not the kind that will qualify you as an amateur Houdini but they are guaranteed to impress even your most skeptical friends.

Solutions are given at the end of the chapter. See how many tricks you can work out yourself before consulting the answers.

TRICKS AND MAGIC

1. The Knife Bridge:

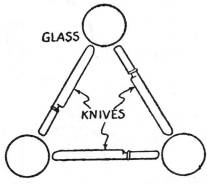

Place three glasses upside down on the table in the corners of a triangle and three knives of the same length between them, forming the sides of the triangle. Be sure that the glasses are one-half inch away from the knife ends. The problem is to form a bridge with the knives, using the glasses as bases, without moving the glasses from their present position.

2. Mysterious Fork:

Prick the tines of a fork with the thumb and index fingers of your right hand. Now with great ceremony place the finger-tips of your free hand on a glass, vase or some other object and draw from it—to the bewilderment of the onlookers—a ringing musical note. Can you discover the trick?

3. Magnetic Spoon:

Pick up a spoon with the thumb on the handle and the middle finger in the bowl.

4.

Draw this diagram without lifting your pencil from the paper, retracing or **crossing** a line.

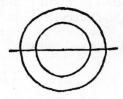

5.

Draw this diagram without lifting your pencil from the paper, retracing or erasing a line.

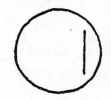

6.

Do the same with this diagram.

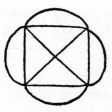

7. Candle Blown Through A Bottle:

Announce that you can blow out a candle through a bottle. Place a lighted candle on a table and about five inches from it place a bottle. Now blow out the candle.

8. Card Magic:

From a deck of cards place five or six Jacks, Kings or Queens on a table in an orderly row. Ask someone to turn some of the cards around while you are out of the room, and when you return you will tell them which cards have been reversed.

9. Magic with a Watch:

Have a player mentally select a number from one through twelve. Tell him to start with the number *above* the number he selected, and count to himself the taps you make on a watch until *he* reaches 20, when he tells you to stop. Now if you know how to do the trick you can announce to the assembled audience the number he selected, and show those near by that the match stick or pencil which you used for tapping is pointing to that number. How is it done?

10. Disappearing Coin:

Ask for a dime and tell the audience you can make it disappear. Put your left elbow on the table and with your right hand rub the dime on your left arm between the elbow and wrist. Drop the dime once with some remark about how small it is; pick it up with the left hand, drop it into your right and continue rubbing. Drop it again with another remark. Pick it up with the *left* hand but *pretend* to drop it into the right, and continue rubbing as before, finishing with an exclamation that it has disappeared. Keep the coin concealed in your left hand, and then with mock surprise make it appear from someone's ear, or mouth.

11. Mathemagic:

Write a whole number of three figures. Now announce that you will reverse the number, and subtracting the lesser from the greater give the answer without hesitating. You can do this by determining the last figure quickly. The middle figure is always nine. Subtract the last figure from nine and you get the first figure and the entire answer. This stunt can be even more mystifying if you give the answer before writing down any figures, and then have someone perform the subtraction on a piece of paper or on the blackboard to check your answer.

$$\begin{array}{r} 532 \\ 235 \\ \hline 297 \end{array}$$

12. The Mysterious Addition:

The trick is to write down the sum of five lines of five figures when you know only the first line. It looks complicated and is always impressive if done with finesse.

Have some person in the group write down the first line for you. Any figure may be used but the last figure on the right cannot be either zero or one. Suppose the person chosen writes down 86215. You can now give the answer, which in this instance will be 286213, regardless of what other four lines are written down later. The first number of the total is always two, the next 4 numbers are the same as the first 4 in the original line, and the last figure is determined by subtracting two from the last figure on the right. In the example given, 5 was the last figure on the right. Subtracting 2 from it, we have 3 and the whole answer: 286213.

But what about the other four lines? How can you be sure they will total this number? To make the trick even more mystifying, ask another person to write down the second line of figures, and just for good measure—the fourth line, also of five figures. You write down the third and fifth lines. But to make the trick work, each figure you write down must total nine when added to the figure directly above. If you are skeptical total the following numbers and see for yourself:

$$
\begin{array}{r}
86215 \\
35206 \\
64793 \\
82143 \\
17856 \\
\hline
286213
\end{array}
$$

13. How to Tell A Person's Age:

Let the person whose age is to be discovered do the figuring. Suppose, for example, that his age is 15 and that he was born in August. Ask him to put down the number of the month in which he was born and proceed as follows:

Number of the month	8
Multiply by two	16
Add five	21
Multiply by fifty	1050
Add the age 15	1065
Subtract 365, leaving	700
Add 115, making	815

The first two figures on the right will always indicate the age and the remaining the month the birthday falls in.

14. How to Tell the Number of Relatives:

Write down the number of brothers (2)	2
Multiply by two	4
Add three	7
Multiply by five	35
Add number of sisters (2)	37
Multiply by ten	370
Add number of grandparents (2)	372
Subtract 150	222

The first figure from left tells the number of brothers, the second the sisters, and the third the grandparents.

15. Match Tricks and Games:

These may be played on hikes and picnics by breaking twigs into a number of sticks of even length.

a. Split the end of match No. 1 and No. 2 slightly and interlock the split ends so the matches are joined firmly. Now place No. 3 match against the other two to form a pyramid which stands alone. The trick is to pick up these three matches using only No. 4 match.

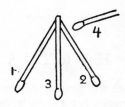

b. Thirteen matches are used in this trick. A man had 6 open front stables for his 6 horses. Thieves tried to steal his horses, and did steal the wall of one stable, so the man used the remaining lumber to make 6 stables with doors for his horses. How did he do it? (Take away one match and make 6 enclosed stables with the remaining 12 matches.)

c. Using 6 matches make 4 equilateral triangles.

d. Using 5 matches form 2 equilateral triangles.

e. Place 7 matches in such a way that 5 matches may be counted crosswise or up and down.

f. Pick up 10 matches by touching only 1 of them.

g. Place 5 matches on a plate. Ask 5 people each to take a match, yet leave 1 on the plate.

h. Use only 9 matches to make 3 squares.

i. If it takes 4 matches to make a square, how many matches to make 2 squares?

j. Arrange 16 matches to form 5 squares in this manner. Now move 3 to new positions so as to bring the number of squares down to 4.

k. Using 8 matches, show that half of 12 is 7.

l. Place 11 matches to form 5 triangles. Remove 3 matches and leave 2 triangles.

m. Place 17 matches in this formation. Two people play. Each draws in turn, taking any number of matches he wishes from *one* row. The object is to make your opponent pick up last match.

n. Using 9 matches, make three dozen. (Do not break the matches.)

MYSTERY GAMES

In these games you need a confederate who knows the trick or system used in each one. He leaves the room, and while he is out the group decides upon some object. When he returns he tells what object was selected without any apparent signal from you or the others. The other players try to guess how the confederate learns which object to pick. When a person thinks he has discovered the trick, he takes the confederate's place. Frequently it develops that the person's idea is all wrong. The confederate then goes out again. If the person is right, however, he may take the confederate's place until someone else guesses the trick.

The Mysterious Cup:

While the confederate is out of the room a coin is placed beneath a cup. Upon returning he touches the bottom of the cup and instantly tells the value of the coin unless it be gold, whereupon he says "gold." The system of signalling is the direction in which the handle of the cup is pointing—one of eight positions—as shown in the diagram.

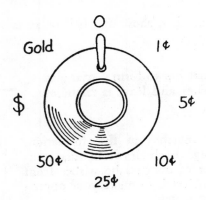

Telepathy:

Place four objects on the floor or table or mark 4 rectangles on the blackboard. While the confederate is out of the room the group selects one of the four objects. The leader then calls the confederate back and tells which object was chosen. He may pretend to take great care, studying each object in detail first. Later he may give the correct one from some distance, even from outside the room, or blindfolded. The signal is given by the leader in re-calling the confederate. Both players have memorized a word or phrase in connection with each article as follows:

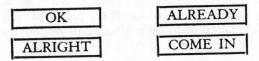

Therefore if the group selects the upper right article, the leader would call "Already" and the confederate upon returning would point or name the upper right hand object.

This and That:

A player and his partner select four objects, two situated above the others, or they place four objects at the corners of a square. Secretly they agree to name these objects as follows:

THIS.	THIS ONE.
THAT.	THAT ONE.

The player then leaves the room or covers his eyes, stating that he will guess which one of the objects the group has chosen. When the choice has been made the partner begins to ask questions. He indicates the right object by using its right name when he points to it. For example, he may point to the upper left object and say, "Is it that?" The player immediately answers, "No," because the right name is "This." His partner next asks, "Is it this one?" pointing to the upper right object. The player replies, "Yes," because his partner named the object by its right name as he pointed to it.

This game may be made more baffling if the player and his partner agree that after a certain number of questions or repetitions of the game the names of the objects shall be reversed. Still later the chosen objects can be indicated by the use of a wrong name instead of the right one.

Red, White and Blue:

While the confederate is out of the room the group selects some object in the room, possibly something worn by one of the players. On the confederate's return the leader points to any object and the confederate says "no" until the right object is pointed out. The signal is given when the leader points to something red. The confederate knows that the next article pointed to will be the one selected by the group. The next time the confederate returns the signal is something white: the third time it is something blue. That is why the game is known to the leader and confederate, but *not* to the group, as "Red, White and Blue." It is similar to, but more complicated than, "Black Magic" in which the signal is to mention something black, just before the correct article.

Jamboree:

As the confederate leaves the room he places four fingers on the door jamb, to signal the leader that he, the confederate, will say "yes" when the leader points to the fourth article. The group then picks any article and the confederate is recalled. The leader having caught his confederate's signal of four fingers on the door jamb points to any three articles asking "Is it this?" "Is it that," and the confederate answers "no," to each. The fourth article pointed to must be the one the group decided on, and when the leader points to it the confederate says, "yes." The signalling should be varied from one to five fingers and be done very unobtrusively.

Tom Thumb:

Three objects are placed in front of the leader, one of which is selected by the group while the confederate is out of the room. Upon returning the latter pretends to make a difficult decision, and then names the correct article. The leader has signalled him with his thumbs. His hands are folded in his lap and very quietly he crosses his right thumb over his left to indicate the article on the right; his left thumb over the right to indicate the article on the left; and his thumbs parallel and together to indicate the center article.

Mind Your Questions:

Place four objects in front of you. Before the game starts, you and your confederate number the articles mentally from one to four. As the game begins, the confederate leaves the room as in the previous game. When the group has selected one of the objects, and the confederate returns, give him the signal by asking any question, starting with a one-letter word if the first object was selected, a two-letter word for the second, a three-letter word for the third, and four-letter word for the fourth.

No Legs to Stand on:

The signal in this game is given by the leader in his first question by indicating whether the object has legs or not. If it has, he mentions from then on only objects which have no legs, until the correct one which has legs. If the article does not have legs, only articles with legs are mentioned after the first one until the article chosen is pointed to. This, of course, is one without legs.

Mental Magic:

The group selects a number while the confederate is out of the room. When he returns, blindfolded if desired, he stands behind the leader, places his hands lightly on the leader's temples or jaws and gets by "mental telepathy" the number chosen. The leader makes the mysterious thought waves by clenching his teeth slightly. This hardens the jaw muscles and causes the temples to swell so that it is easy for the confederate to guess the number selected. If the number is 621, the leader clenches his jaws six times, pauses, clenches them twice, pauses, and then clenches them once. Zero is indicated by ten presses.

Secret Signals:

A different type of mystery game can be played by secretly choosing a confederate whom the gathering does not suspect of being "in cahoots" with you. The signals are made in plain view so they must be casual and unobtrusive. One of the most effective is to have the confederate smoke a cigarette. The cigarette in the right corner of his mouth means the right article, in the left corner the article on the left, and if the confederate doesn't put the cigarette to his mouth at all, the center article. Or the leader can guess whether cards are red or black by similar signals from his confederate.

Signals can also be given by clasping hands or moving the hands or feet in a prescribed manner. These signals can be very deceiving if the movements are natural to the confederate.

SOLUTIONS

1. Place the flexible blade tips together, under one knife and over the other, so that they remain firmly together. Then place each knife handle on a glass.

2. Placing your free hand on some object—and perhaps giving a talk on magic while you are doing so—is only for effect. The trick is done with your other hand. Lower the fork to the table as soon as the tines have been pricked. The table acts as a sounding board and allows the note from the makeshift tuning fork to be heard.

3. First rub your finger and thumb on the table cloth to remove all grease and moisture.

   4.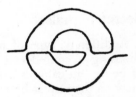

5. Turn a small corner of your paper towards you. Draw a horizontal line on the main part of the paper till it meets the point of the turned-down corner. It should be the same length as the line in the diagram. Continue the line along the corner. This should not show on the large sheet, but should equal the distance between the line in the circle and the circumference. Now turn your pencil off the corner and away from it. Start drawing the circle. When you come to the corner, turn it back and complete the circle.

6. Fold a piece of paper in half. From the edge where the fold is, fold the paper again but this time turn the paper only about a half inch. Now along the edge of the second fold draw a line about an inch long in the center of the paper so that it

makes two lines with one stroke, one on the fold, the other on the main part of the paper. To do this a soft pencil should be used. Keeping the pencil on the paper, unfold the paper and complete the diagram.

7. When you blow be sure your mouth is about 6 inches from the bottle and on a level with the candle flame. The round bottle will divide the air current, which unites on the opposite side and blows out the flame.

8. Notice that the cards have a wider margin at one end. When you place them on the table, have all the wide margins nearest you. Then when you return to the room it is a simple matter to see which cards now have narrow margins nearest you.

9. You tap at random for seven taps, but on the *eighth* tap touch 12 on the watch, on the *ninth* tap touch 11 and so on, going around the watch face backwards. When the player stops you, your pointer will be touching the number he had selected mentally.

15. *a.* Carefully slide No. 4 well under No. 3, so the ends are beyond No. 1 and No. 2 slightly, so the pyramid falls with No. 3 falling on No. 4, under No. 1 and No. 2. Now raise No. 4 slowly so No. 3 is wedged between No. 4 and No. 1 and No. 2, and all three may be lifted.

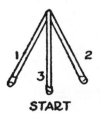

START

NO.4 SLIDES IN

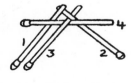

NO.3 DROPS UNDER
(IS WEDGED IN)
NO.4 PICKS UP ALL

b. Six enclosed stables with 12 matches.

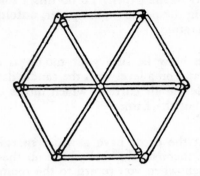

c. Place three on table to form triangle. Now hold three in place above them to form equilateral pyramid.

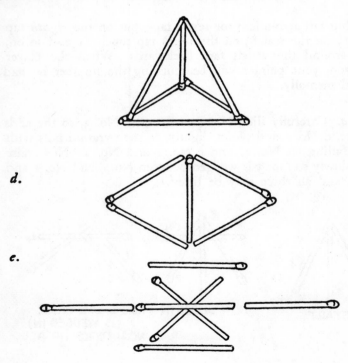

d.

e.

f.

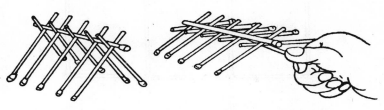

Start   Finish

g. The last person to pick up a match takes plate and all.

h.

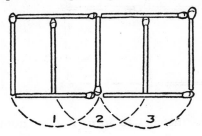

i. Seven matches.

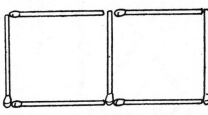

l.

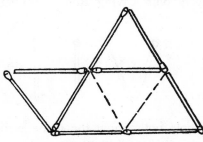

j.

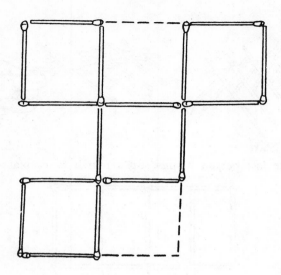

k. Place eight matches to form Roman numeral 12.

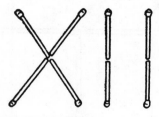

Now remove half leaving Roman numeral 7.

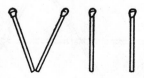

m. If two people both know the game well, the one who starts has the best chance of winning.

n.

CHAPTER SIX

Charades and Stunts

Producing Charades:

Those who are unacquainted with the fun involved in charades and stunts will find much satisfaction by building these in committees for parties or other social gatherings.

Select a word with dramatic possibility and develop a pantomime around it. Endeavor to have all speaking and acting closely related to the word so as to avoid confusion in interpretation. The most simple words sometimes are difficult to understand, especially so if the pantomime is too elaborate. Bear in mind these simple principles: Use words common to the audience. Interpret each syllable dramatically, permit no charade to exist beyond three minutes, and pantomime no more than four words at any one program or party.

Example of A Charade:

Animate ...."Anne-I-mate!"

The setting may be in a home where a lively family argument is in progress relative to a son's marriage. To each objection the son emphatically replies, "Anne I mate."

Antic ...."Aunt!" "Hic!"

Stage setting, a room. A woman is under influence of liquor. A bottle may be on the table. A much concerned individual frantically tries to revive the woman from her stupor, as she says, "Aunt!" The woman only replies with "Hic!"

A few suggestions follow:

Anneal ...."An eel!" (Fisherman's return.)
Announce ...."An ounce." (Store scene.)
Antecedent ...."Aunty, see dent."

Batter ...."Bat her!" (Baseball or family row.)
Cantilever ...."Can't he leave her?" (Gossip.)
Party ....Part-tea.
Handicap ....Handy-cap.
Pasteboard ....Paste-board.
Pastime ....Past-time.
Stationary ....Station-airy.

Group Charades:

Divide the guests into groups. Each group selects its own word and pantomimes it. The opponents are supposed to guess the word. A prize may be awarded to the group producing the most humorous charade.

Current-Event Charades:

Select a recent event and dramatize it.

Historical Charades:

Dramatize an historical event.

Popular-Book Charades:

Take a title, as, "Gone With the Wind," and dramatize it.

Name Charades:

Dramatize the given and surname of one or more persons attending the party.

Community Charades:

Dramatize a local group, as Board of Education, street, park, or store names may be dramatized. But do not combine features. Select one phase, announce it and dramatize it; either streets, or parks, or stores, or local groups.

Poetic Charades:

Select a group, as the New England Poets, and dramatize several of their names. Titles of poems may be pantomimed.

Literary Charades:

Announce an author or source and dramatize well-known statements, but only one statement at a time.

Popular Song Charades:

Select a group of songs, as Negro Spirituals, songs of Stephen Foster, etc., and build charades around one verse.

Radio Charades:

Select the names of prominent radio stars, or radio advertisements, and build charades around them.

Nature Lore Charades:

Select one subject of nature lore, as rocks, trees, animals, birds, flowers, or natural formations, and dramatize.

Other Suggestions Are:

Names of our Presidents, cities, states; names of our children, wives or husbands; hobbies of the group, and favorite expressions of individual members.

Suggestions for Stunts:

When the desire is to produce more elaborate stunts than those put on by teams at a party without preparation, detailed planning should be made accordingly, in advance of the party.

These simple suggestions should be followed:

FIRST, for special occasions the stunts should be in keeping with the event. If the party is patriotic the stunt should be patriotic; if a pre-nuptial event, the stunt should be the same.

SECOND, the game leader or the recreational committee should willingly bear censure for being too meticulous rather than for being shoddy or indifferent to results. Lengthly rehearsals are not necessary. But planning should be such as to produce precision of movement, clarity of voice and familiarity with one's part so as to avoid being out of character.

THIRD, all materials and costumes should be acquired at the lowest cost. In the average community there are garments which may be borrowed. Often with a little ingenuity old-fashioned or special costumes may be adapted at a very low cost. Where new material must be purchased cambric generally serves the purpose. Raw wool dyed to the desired color, or crepe hair, built on a stocking foundation will suffice for the average male wig. Crepe hair attached to the face after an application of Spirit Gum, affords effective beards, goatees and sideburns, and are much cheaper than manufactured or rented articles. Discarded hair switches and other *coiffure* of the older generation obtain for women extra hair effects. As a rule, improvised, inexpensive costumes and make-up supervised by a talented person of the community will answer for the average stunt if the stage lights are not too brilliant.

Suggestions for make-up may be obtained through the purchase of an inexpensive pamphlet at a costuming shop, or by consulting books on that subject in the city library.

In each community are persons with fair or special talents who desire attention: musicians, readers, humorists, etc. The alert leader will use these people. Under capable direction an amateur occasionally surprises his closest friends. Even the aged who have been given opportunity to develop their own stunts have produced remarkable results with old-time dancing, music and historical skits.

> We are born with faculties and powers capable almost of any-thing—such at least as would carry us further than can easily be imagined; but it is only the exercise of those powers which gives us ability and skill in anything, and leads us toward perfection.
> **John Locke**

CHAPTER SEVEN

Games for Little Tots

Charley over the Water:

A circle is formed. The players join hands and dance around "Charley" who is "IT," as they sing:

Charley over the water,
Charley over the sea;
Charley catch a blackbird,
But he can't catch me.

On the word "me", each player stoops to a squatting position. If Charley tags one before that person is fully squatted he becomes Charley and the former Charley joins the circle.

Farmer in the Dell:

The children form a circle and sing the following. A child is "IT" in the center of the circle. At the beginning of the second verse, "IT" steps forward and draws a player into the circle. The player chosen draws in turn a player to the inside from the circle, until the "cheese" is taken in the eighth verse. That person becomes the farmer, and the game is continued.

1—The farmer in the dell,
The farmer in the dell,
Heigh ho the derry oh,
The farmer in the dell.

2—The farmer takes a wife,
The farmer takes a wife,
Heigh ho the derry oh,
The farmer takes a wife.

86

3—The wife takes the child, etc.

4—The child takes the nurse, etc.

5—The nurse takes the dog, etc.

6—The dog takes the cat, etc.

7—The cat takes the rat, etc.

8—The rat takes the cheese, etc.

9—The cheese stands alone, etc.

Hide and Seek:

"IT" counts to one hundred at a goal while the other players hide. Then he seeks the hidden players, as they try to keep out of sight and count themselves in at the goal without being tagged, crying, "One, two, three for myself." A person tagged becomes "IT."

Itiskit, Itaskit:

A circle is formed with "IT" walking on the outside with a handkerchief, as the players sing:

> Itisket, Itasket,—
> A green and yellow basket;
> I wrote a letter to my love,
> And on the way I dropped it,—
> I dropped it, I dropped it;
> A little doggie picked it up,
> And put it in his pocket,—
> His pocket, his pocket.

On the words "dropped it," "IT" is supposed to drop the handkerchief behind a player, as he continues to walk around the circle. The person behind whom it is dropped must chase "IT" and try to tag him before he gets to the vacant place in the circle. Should the person behind whom the handkerchief was dropped fail to realize the handkerchief is at his heels, when "IT" reaches him, he tags him on the back and compels him to go to the center of the circle and remain there until he can run into a vacant place in the circle. The object is for the chaser to tag the person who is "IT" and become "IT" himself.

In and out the Window:

A circle is formed and a person is chosen to be "IT." "IT" winds in and out around the persons in the circle during the singing of the first verse. During the second and third verses "IT" and the chosen person pantomime the words. At the conclusion of the third verse the chosen person becomes "IT."

> 1—Go in and out the window,
> Go in and out the window,
> Go in and out the window,
> As we have done before.

> 2—Go kneel before your lover, etc.,
> For he has won the day.

> 3—Now bow before you leave her, etc.,
> And go upon your way.

The Mulberry Bush:

A circle is formed. The players join hands and dance or run around in circle formation singing during the first verse. At the beginning of the second and each subsequent verse the players stand still, dramatizing the words. The seventh verse is dramatized by joining hands again and swinging the arms. The players make a right face and begin walking in circle formation during the last verse.

> 1—Here we go round the mulberry bush,
> The mulberry bush, the mulberry bush;
> Here we go round the mulberry bush,
> On a cold and wintry morning.

2—This is the way we wash our clothes, etc.,
So early Monday morning.

3—This is the way we iron our clothes, etc.,
So early Tuesday morning.

4—This is the way we scrub the floor, etc.,
So early Wednesday morning.

5—This is the way we darn our socks, etc.,
So early Thursday morning.

6—This is the way we sweep the floor, etc.,
So early Friday morning.

7—Thus we play when work is done, etc.,
So early Saturday morning.

8—This is the way we go to church, etc.,
So early Sunday morning.

Puss in A Corner:

The players select goals or bases from which they endeavor to move without being tagged. The object is for "IT" to tag a player off base. The person tagged becomes "IT." "IT" may steal any vacant base. A player forced off a base by another player, after "IT" has secured a "corner" becomes "IT."

Statues:

A line of players is established behind the one who is "IT." As he counts to a determined number the players rush as close as possible to him and establish individual poses. Should the one who is "IT" see a player step or move after he has quickly turned around, that person becomes "IT."

This method of playing "Statues" is equally as old, more fascinating, and less dangerous than that of swinging the partner, as in Crack the Whip," and taking the pose thereafter.

CHAPTER EIGHT

Songs for Group Singing and Musical Games

Polly-Wolly Doodle:

1—Oh, I went down South to see my Sal,
Sing Polly-wolly doodle all the day;
My Sally am a spunky girl,
Sing Polly-wolly doodle all the day.

CHORUS:

Fare thee well, fare thee well,
Fare thee well, my fair fay,
For I'm going to Louisiana,
For to see my Susianna,
Sing Polly-wolly doodle all the day.

2—Oh, my Sal, she am a maiden fair, etc.
With curly eyes and laughing hair, etc.

———

3—Oh, I came to a river, an' I couldn't get across, etc.
An' jumped upon a nigger, an' thot he was a hoss, etc.

———

4—Oh, a grass-hopper sittin' on a railroad track, etc.
A-pickin' his teef wid a carpet tack, etc.

———

5—Oh, I went to bed, but it wasn't no use, etc.
My feet stuck out for a chicken roost, etc.

———

6—Behind de barn, down on my knees, etc.
I thought I heard a chicken sneeze, etc.

7—He sneezed so hard wid de 'hoppin' cough, etc.
He sneezed his head an' his tail right off, etc.

Anon

Juanita:

Soft o'er the fountain,
Lingering falls the southern moon;
Far o'er the mountain,
Breaks the day too soon!
On thy dark eyes splendor,
Where the warm light loves to dwell,
Weary looks, yet tender,
Speaks their fond farewell.
Nita! Juanita!
Ask they soul if we should part!
Nita! Juanita!
Lean thou on my heart.

Mrs. Horton

Good Night, Ladies:

1—Good night, ladies!
Good night, ladies!
Good night, ladies!
We're going to leave you now.

CHORUS:

Merrily we roll along,
Roll along, roll along,
Merrily we roll along,
O'er the dark blue sea.

2—Farewell, ladies! etc.

3—Sweet dreams, ladies! etc.

Anon

The Quilting Party:

1—In the sky the bright stars glittered,
    On the bank the pale moon shone;
And 'twas from Aunt Dinah's quilting party,
    I was seeing Nellie home.

CHORUS:

    I was seeing Nellie home,
    I was seeing Nellie home,
    And 'twas from Aunt Dinah's quilting party,
    I was seeing Nellie home.

2—On my life new hopes were dawning,
    And those hopes have lived and grown;
And 'twas from Aunt Dinah's quilting party,
    I was seeing Nellie home.

Anon

Comin' Thro' the Rye:

If a body meet a body,
    Comin' thro' the rye,
If a body kiss a body,
    Need a body cry?

Ev'ry lassie has her laddie,
    Nane they say ha'e I;
Yet a' the lads they smile on me,
    When comin' thro' the rye.

Robert Burns

Tavern in the Town:

There is a tavern in the town, in the town,
And there my true love sits him down, sits him down,
And takes his ease 'mid laughter free
And never, never thinks of me, thinks of me.
Fare thee well, for I must leave thee,

Do not let the parting grieve thee,
And remember that the best of friends must part.
Adieu, adieu, kind friends, adieu, adieu, adieu,
I can no longer stay with you, stay with you,
I'll hang my harp on a weeping willow tree,
And may the world go well with thee.

Anon

Beautiful Dreamer:

Beautiful dreamer, wake unto me,
Starlight and dewdrops are waiting for thee,
Sounds of the rude world, heard in the day,
Lull'd by the moonlight have all passed away!
Beautiful dreamer, queen of my song,
List while I woo thee, with soft melody;
Gone are the cares of life's busy throng,
Beautiful dreamer, awake unto me!
Beautiful dreamer, awake unto me!

Stephen Foster

Old Folks at Home:

1—'Way down upon de Swanee River,
    Far, far away,
Dere's wha' my heart is turning ebber,
    Dere's wha' de old folks stay.

All up an' down de whole creation
    Sadly I roam,
Still longin' for de old plantation,
    An' for de old folks at home.

CHORUS:

All de world am sad and dreary
    Eb'ry where I roam;
Oh! darkies, how my heart grows weary,
    Far from de old folks at home.

2—One little hut among de bushes,
    One dat I love,
Still sadly to my mem'ry rushes,
    No matter where I rove.
When will I see de bees a hummin'
    All roun' de comb?
When will I hear de banjo tummin'
    Down in my good old home?

Stephen C. Foster

John Brown's Baby:

John Brown's baby had a cold upon its chest;
John Brown's baby had a cold upon its chest;
John Brown's baby had a cold upon its chest,
So they rubbed it with camphorated oil.

Anon

This song may be used as a circle or line game. In whatever way it is used, either as a game or a diversion during an elaborate social function, much enjoyment will result by watching the laughable motions of others.

As a line or circle game, persons failing to make the proper motions or singing the word instead of making the required motion, are eliminated.

The first round of this verse is sung as it stands. From the second to the sixth repetition a word is omitted each time and substituted for a motion. The omission of the previous singing is repeated and carried into each successive repetition, from the omission of "baby" to that of "camphorated oil." The second time the verse is sung the word "baby" is omitted and substituted for a rocking motion executed by placing the right hand on the left elbow and the left hand on the upper right arm. The third time "cold" is omitted and substituted for a cough. Then "chest" is left out for a pat on the chest with the open palm. Next, "rubbed" is substituted for a rubbing motion. Lastly, a sniff is made instead of singing the words "camphorated oil".

Single Circle Games:

JOLLY IS THE MILLER

Jolly is the miller and he lives by the mill,
The wheel goes around with a right good will,
One hand in the hopper and the other in the sack,
The wheel goes on and we all turn back.

Jolly is the miller and he lives by the mill,
The wheel goes around with a right good will,
One hand in the hopper and the other in the sack,
And the ladies go forward and the men turn back.

Raining, hailing, cold stormy weather,
I have no shoes and I have no leather,
You be the reaper, I'll be the binder,
I've lost my true love and here shall I find her.

The above and following Singing Games to and including "Oh!
Susanna" are from "Planned Games for the Social Hour" (A circular
of the Division of Rural Life, and Farm Population, U. S. Dept. of
Agriculture) by Ella Gardner.

Partners stand side by side, boys on the girls' left, in a circle with their hands joined behind them in skating position.

During the first three lines of the first verse they skip or walk around the circle counter-clockwise. On the last line of the verse, they reverse, turning back to back without letting go of hands and walk clockwise through the first three lines of the second verse.

On the fourth line, partners drop hands and the boys turn around, walking in the opposite direction to the girls. This continues through verse three until the last one when the boys take the girls nearest to them, turn them around to walk counter-clockwise and the game begins again.

THE NEEDLE'S EYE

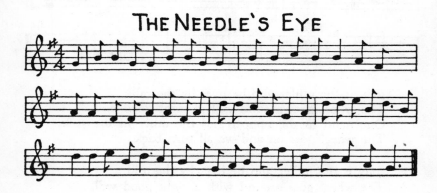

The needle's eye it doth supply
The thread that runs so truly,
There's many a lass that I let pass
Because I wanted you
Because I wanted you
Because I wanted you
There's many a lass that I let pass
Because I wanted you.

One or more couples form bridges. The rest of the group marches under them until the words "Because I wanted you" in line 4. At this point the player on the inside of the bridge takes the hand of one of the line nearest to him and turns him into the circle while the other person in the bridge joins the line of marchers. New partners are not chosen at the end of the verse but in the middle only.

SKIP TO MY LOU

CHORUS: Skip, skip, skip, to my Lou,
Skip, skip, skip to my Lou,
Skip, skip, skip to my Lou,
Skip to my Lou, my darlin'.

Little red wagon, painted blue (etc.)
Chorus.
Dad's ol' hat got tore in two (etc.)
Chorus.
Purty as a redbird, purtier too (etc.)
Chorus.
Can't git a redbird, a bluebird'll do (etc.)
Chorus.
She is gone and I'll go too (etc.)
Chorus.
Git me another'n as purty as you (etc.)

Chorus.

Formation:

After choosing partners, the players form a single large circle, girls on boys' right.
Game: .
An odd man starts the game by skipping to a girl, crossing hands with her and skipping around the circle and back to

her place with her. As soon as his partner has left him, the deserted boy starts out to get another and so the game goes on indefinitely.

TURN THE GLASSES OVER

I've been to Haar-lem, I've been to Do-ver, I've trav-eled this wide world all o-ver, O-ver, o-ver, three times o-ver, Drink all the spring wa-ter Turn the glasses o-ver, Sail-ing east, Sail-ing west, Sail-ing o-ver the o-cean, Bet-ter watch out when the boat be-gins to rock or you'll lose your girl in the o-cean.

Players stand side by side in a circle of partners, boys on the inside, girls on their right. Crossed hands are joined in skating position. Extra boys or girls are in the middle.

A. Partners walk around the circle until the words "Turn the glasses over", when they wring the dishrag and let go of hands.

B. Boys walk the opposite direction, girls continue walking as they were. Extras fall into line. On the word "lose" each boy takes the girl nearest to him. Extras go in the middle and the game starts again.

PUSH THE BUSINESS ON

I'll buy a horse and steal a gig,
And all the world shall have a jig,
And I'll do all that ever I can
To push the business on,
To push the business on,
And I'll do all that ever I can,
To push the business on.

Partners stand side by side in a single circle, girls on partner's right. All hold hands.

1-6   Slide step around circle to right.

7-8   Drop hands, each player turns in place clapping his hands.

9-10   Partners face, clap own hands once, partner's once and own hands again.

11-14   Partners join right hands and skip once, around each other then half way around again, leaving the girl in the boy's place. This gives everyone a new partner with whom to repeat the game.

THERE IS SOMEBODY WAITING

1—There is somebody waiting
There is somebody waiting
There is somebody waiting
For me.

2—Take the two, leave the others
Take the two, leave the others
Take the two, leave the others
For me.

3—Swing the one, leave the other
Swing the one, leave the other
Swing the one, leave the other
For me.

This game is played in a single circle. An odd player stands in the center while verse one is sung. During verse two the player, if she is a girl, chooses two boys and walks around in a small circle with them. During verse three, she leaves one of the boys and swings the other back into the big circle. The boy who is left then plays the game with two girls and so it continues.

Oh! Susanna:

1—I came from Alabama with
My banjo on my knee,
I'm goin' to Lou'siana,
My true love for to see.

It rained all night the day I left,
The weather it was dry;
The sun so hot I froze to death;
Susanna, don't you cry.

CHORUS:

> Oh Susanna, oh, don't you cry for me,
> For I'm goin' to Lou'siana with my banjo on my knee.

2—I had a dream the other night,
> When everything was still;
> I thought I saw Susanna
> A-coming down the hill.

> The buckwheat cake was in her mouth,
> The tear was in her eye;
> Says I, I'm coming from the South,
> Susanna, don't you cry.

Stephen C. Foster

*GAME: *Oh Susanna.*

Formation:

In couples, standing in a large circle, facing in.

Action:

"I came from Alabama (men march 4 steps toward center)
With my banjo on my knee (move back 4 steps to places)
I'm g'wan to Louisiana (ladies do likewise)
My true love for to see. (Return to place, then face partner
and give him right hand.)
It rained all night the day I left (Grand right and left to
end of verse)
The weather it was dry
De sun so hot I froze myself,
Susanna, don't you cry." (On words "cry" get new partner
and face to promenade counter-clockwise.)

Chorus:

(Promenade with new partner)
"Oh, Susanna, oh, don't you cry for me
For I'm goin' to Lou'siana
Wid my banjo on my knee." (On last word face center to
repeat all.)

*The game "Oh Susanna" was arranged by Miss Ella Gardner for
"Planned Games for the Social Hour," previously mentioned.

America:

1—My country! tis' of thee,
Sweet land of liberty,
    Of thee I sing;
Land where my fathers died,
Land of the pilgrim's pride,
From every mountain side,
    Let freedom ring!

2—My native country, thee,
Land of the noble free,
    Thy name I love;
I love thy rocks and rills,
Thy woods and templed hills;
My heart with rapture thrills,
    Like that above.

3—Let music swell the breeze,
And ring from all the trees
    Sweet freedom's song;
Let mortal tongues awake;
Let all that breathe partake;
Let rocks their silence break,
    The sound prolong.

4—Our father's God, to thee,
Author of liberty,
    To thee we sing;
Long may our land be bright
With freedom's holy light;
Protect us by thy might,
    Great God our King.

*5—Now may the God above
Guard the dear lands we love;
    Or East or West;
Let love more fervent glow,

As peaceful ages go,
And strength more stronger grow,
Blessings and blest.

*AMERICA by Samuel F. Smith, The INTERNATIONAL HYMN, one verse attached,—written by Prof. George Huntington. Included in recognition of the common bonds between Canada and the United States of America, and all Democracies.

My Bonnie:

My Bonnie lies over the ocean,
My Bonnie lies over the sea;
My Bonnie lies over the ocean,
Oh, bring back my Bonnie to me.

CHORUS:

Bring back, bring back,
Bring back my Bonnie to me, to me;
Bring back, bring back,
Oh, bring back my Bonnie to me.

Anon

All Through the Night:

1—Sleep, my child, and peace attend thee
All through the night;
Guardian angels God will send thee,
All through the night,
Soft the drowsy hours are creeping,
Hill and vale in slumber steeping,
I my loving vigil keeping
All through the night.

2—While the moon her watch is keeping
All through the night;
While the weary world is sleeping
All through the night.

O'er thy spirit gently stealing,
Visions of delight revealing,
    Breathes a pure and holy feeling,
All through the night.

Anon

Auld Lang Syne:

Should auld acquaintance be forgot,
    And never brought to mind?
Should auld acquaintance be forgot,
    And days of auld lang syne?

CHORUS:

For auld lang syne, my dear,
    For auld lang syne;
We'll tak' a cup o' kindness yet
    For auld lang syne.

Robert Burns

CHAPTER NINE

Skill Games

These games have been taken from the Handbook for Recreation Leaders by Ella Gardner, Publication No. 231 of the Children's Bureau, U. S. Department of Labor, and are used by permission.

Badminton:

For this game a court 18 by 19 feet in size should be laid out as indicated in the diagram. Jumping standards may be used as temporary posts to hold the net. A regulation tennis

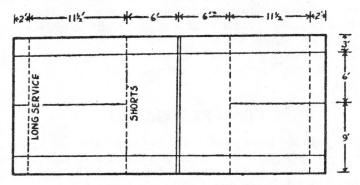

net may be used, or a clothesline or twine may be wound tightly back and forth between the posts.

Long-handled rackets are used, and a feathered shuttlecock or "bird." A sponge or a ball of yarn or rubber makes a satisfactory substitute for the shuttlecock. The sponge should be trimmed down with scissors until it is about 3 inches in diameter and fairly round. The yarn ball should be about 2 inches

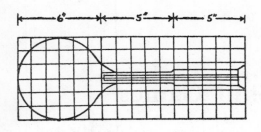

in diameter, wound tightly enough to be firm but not hard. The rubber ball should not be more than 1¼ inches in diameter (a jacks ball is excellent) and should be tied in the middle of an 8-inch square of muslin. Substitutes for the regulation racket may be made of 3-ply material with a round head 6 inches in diameter and a 10-inch handle, of the shape shown in the illustration.

The game may be played by two or four players. The first service and each beginning service thereafter starts in the right half of the court and alternates to left and right as long as the serving side continues to score. The server stands in his half court and strikes the "bird" with an underhand stroke, trying to place it in the opposite half court. It is volleyed back and forth as in Lawn Tennis until it lands on the court, goes out of bounds, or strikes the net.

Only the serving players may score. Fifteen or twenty-one points or "aces" constitute a game, and three games make a rubber.

BEAN-BAG GAMES

Bean bags are easily made from canvas or other strong cloth. They may be square, oblong, or round and may vary in size. Six inches square is a convenient dimension. The bag should be filled slightly more than half full of beans.

Bean-Bag Shuffle:

For this game a few shot may be put with the beans to add weight to the bags. The players slide the bean bags along the floor with the motion used in bowling. The floor chart and the method of scoring are the same as described for Shuffleboard.

Bean-Bag Board:

A board about 2 feet wide and 2½ or 3 feet long should have holes cut in it to represent eyes, nose, and mouth, as is  shown in the illustration. The eyes should be about 7 inches long and 5 inches wide, the mouth about 4 inches long and 10 inches wide, and the base of the triangle for the nose about 8 inches long. The board can be placed against a wall or fence or supported by a hinged prop. The players stand at a line 10 to 15 feet from the board. Each player has five bean bags, or five may be used by the entire group playing in turn.

A bag thrown into the mouth counts 5 points; one into the nose, 10 points; one into an eye, 20 points. The player who first scores 100 wins the game; or the player having the highest score after all have finished four turns may be considered the winner.

For a large number of players it is desirable to have more than one board, so that the players may be divided into several groups and the game be made faster.

Duck on Rock:

Each player is provided with a bean bag, which is called his duck. A large rock or a post is chosen as the duck rock, and 25 feet from it a line is drawn. A guard is selected by having all the players throw their ducks from this line, the one whose duck falls nearest the rock to become the first guard. He lays his duck on this rock and stands by it. The other players then stand behind the line and take turns in throwing their ducks at the duck on the rock, trying to knock it off. After each throw a player must recover his own duck and run home (back of the line). If he is tagged by the guard while trying to do this, he must change places with the guard. The guard may tag him whenever he is in front of the line, unless he stands with his foot on his own duck where it fell. He may stand thus as long as he wishes, awaiting opportunity to run home; but the moment he lifts his duck from the ground or takes his foot from it, he may be tagged. Furthermore, he is not allowed to lay his duck on the ground again after he has once lifted it to run with it.

The guard must not tag any player unless his own duck is on the rock. If it has been knocked off, he must pick it up and replace it before he may chase anyone. This replacing gives the thrower who knocked it off some time to recover his own duck and run home. As long as the guard's duck stays on the rock, several throwers may have to wait before they can try to recover their ducks.

A player tagged by the guard must put his own duck on the rock and become guard. The one who is no longer guard must get his duck from the rock and run for the line as quickly as possible, because he can now be tagged as soon as the new duck is on the rock.

If a duck falls very near the rock without displacing the guard's duck, the guard may challenge its thrower by calling, "Span!" This gives him time to measure with his hand the distance between the rock and that duck. If the distance is shown to be less than a span (the distance from the end of the thumb to the end of the little finger), the thrower must change places with the guard as if he had been tagged.

Shuffleboard:

Shuffleboard is played by two teams of two players each. It can be either a floor game or a table game. For the floor game the diagram may be drawn on a porch floor or attic floor as is shown in the illustration. Each team has three wooden disks 3 inches in diameter and 1 inch thick. The shovels may be made by attaching old broom handles to pieces of wood cut out to fit the disks.

For the table game the lines may be drawn on a piece of composition board or a table, with the dimensions reduced to about one-fourth of the size for the floor game. The shovel should be about 12 inches long, and checkers or buttons can be used for the disks.

One player from each team stands back of the "10-off" space at each end. The first player shoves one of his disks toward the opposite end, trying to make it stop on a high number on

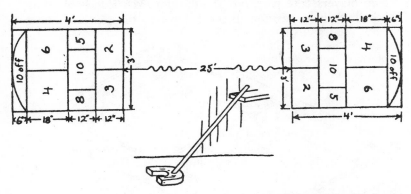

his opponent's side. If the head of his shovel passes the back line of the diagram, the play does not count. A member of the other team makes the next turn, and this continues until each player has played three times. Each one tries to dislodge his opponent's disks as well as to place his own. If a disk touches the line, it does not count.

At the end of the round each player counts up the total of the numbers on which his disks rest, and the players at the opposite end begin to play.

Box Hockey:

This very active game, which may be played indoors or out, requires a space about 15 feet square. A frame or box 3 feet wide and 8 feet long should be made, with a center board set securely across the middle. Lumber about 1 inch thick and about 9 inches wide should be used. The corners of the box should be reinforced by blocks to which the boards can be screwed. An opening about 4 inches wide and 3 inches high should be cut in the middle of each end, and two such openings in the middle board, as is shown in the illustration. In the top of the center board a notch is cut about 2 inches wide and 1 inch deep.

Hockey or shinny sticks are used, and a puck. For the puck a wooden disk 1¾ inches in diameter or an old baseball or small croquet ball may be used.

Two players take part, one standing at each side of the box. The ball is set in position in the notch and the players "knock

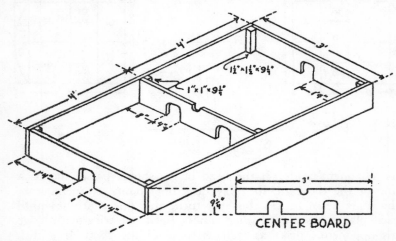

CENTER BOARD

off" as in hockey; that is, they touch their sticks to the floor or ground, then strike them together three times above the ball. Immediately both strike at the ball, each player trying to push it into his opponent's section of the box, then outside the box through the hole in the end of that section, which is his goal. The player in whose section the ball lands must get it into his opponent's section through one of the openings in the middle board before he can try for the goal. If a ball is knocked outside the box it is brought back to the place from which it started and put into play from there.

Five points constitute a game. A point is scored each time the ball goes through a goal. It is considered through if it has gone far enough to clear the inside edge of the box.

Horseshoe Pitching:

The game of Horseshoe Pitching is widely known and very generally enjoyed. The stakes over which the horseshoes are to be pitched should be 8 inches above the ground. The regulation distance apart is 40 feet, but for young players this may be reduced to 30 feet or even less. Two or four players may take part. If there are four, they play in two teams, with team mates standing at opposite stakes. Each player (or each team) has two horseshoes, and they take turns pitching them.

The game consists of 50 points. If a player rings the stake with one of his horseshoes, he scores 3 points. If both of his horseshoes ring it, he scores 6 points. Points are awarded also for putting horseshoes near the stake, the nearest one scoring 1 point. If both the nearest ones belong to one player, he scores 2 points. A combination of one "ringer" and the nearest horseshoe scores 4 points. Only one player scores in a turn; if both make "ringers," each cancels the other. If the horseshoes of opponents are equidistant from the stake, no points are awarded for either of them. First play in the next turn is given to the member of the winning team at the opposite stake.

Horseshoes and stakes made especially for the game may be purchased. A copy of the official rules is usually packed with each pair of such horseshoes.

Barrel-Hoop Quoits:

A quoit game similar to that in which horseshoes are used may be played with barrel hoops. The stakes over which the hoops are to be tossed should be about 2 feet above the ground and 15 feet apart. One point is awarded each time the hoop rings the stake.

Piercing the Hoop:

A barrel hoop is suspended from the branch of a tree. The players stand on a line about 20 feet away and try to throw a fishing pole or light 10-foot rod through this hoop. Each contestant has five trials, and a point is scored each time the rod goes through the hoop. The throwing line may be put farther back when the players are expert.

Barrel Toss:

The players stand about 20 feet away from a barrel and try to throw stones or wooden blocks into it. Each may have five throws, and a point may be awarded for each stone or block that goes in. The throwing line may be put farther back when the players are expert.

Clock Golf:

The game of Clock Golf is played in a circle 15 to 40 feet in diameter, numbered around its circumference like a clock face. A putting hole 4 inches in diameter and 4 inches deep is played anywhere within this circle. Instead of golf sticks, tree branches that have knots at suitable angles may be used. The players one after the other putt from each of the figures on the circle. The object is to "hole out" in the smallest number of strokes.

Obstacle Golf:

Obstacle-golf courses can be made by the use of tin cans, bent-tin tunnels, mounds, and small trenches. The advantage of this game is that it can be played in a small space.

If a large lawn is available, many other kinds of competitive games with golf balls and clubs can be worked out. A series of tin cans about 4 inches in diameter can be sunk to form the putting green. Sand greens which the wind and rain cannot easily carry away can be made by mixing the sand for a thin top layer with oil drained from the crank case of an automobile.

Miss the Bell:

A bell is suspended in a hoop about 8 inches in diameter, and a small ball is given to the players. They take turns tossing the ball, trying to send it through the hoop without causing the bell to ring. One point is scored each time the ball goes through, and three points are scored if the bel does not ring.

Jar-Ring Toss:

A board about 28 inches square is prepared by driving 23 nails 3 inches long partly into it at an angle, or by screwing into it little right-angle hooks like those used to hold curtain rods. Each hook is given a value, as is shown in the accom-

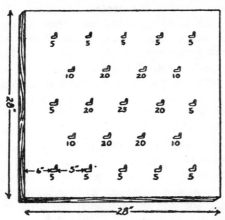

panying illustr a t i o n. Figures can be cut from a calendar and pasted on. The board may be hung against the wall or set on a table. Its center should be about shoulder high. The players stand 10 feet from the board. Each is given 12 rubber jar rings, which he tries to toss so that they will hang on the nails or hooks having the highest numbers. The players throw three times in a play and rotate four times. It is well to mark the rings with crayon or paint so that each person may identify his own in counting the final score.

Croquet:

The regulation croquet court is 30 by 60 feet, but the game can be adapted to the available space. Either a grass or a dirt court may be used. The game is played by two to eight players. Croquet sets may be secured at reasonable prices in toy and sport shops; a set of rules comes with the equipment. Mallets may be improvised from old stair rails or other lumber, wickets from heavy wire; and old baseballs or other hard balls may be used.

Croquet-Ball Bowling:

Blocks of wood or tin cans may be set up for tenpins, and croquet balls may be used for bowling. A smooth floor or smooth level piece of ground is needed. One point is scored for every tenpin that falls, and 15 points are scored if all fall at one shot.

Marble Bowling.

Ten nails about an inch long are arranged like tenpins, a full inch apart, on a table at least 4 feet long. Three marbles are given to each player. In bowling with these the players must have their knuckles on a line 3 feet away from the nearest row of nails. The distance may be made greater or less according to the skill of the players. One point is scored for every nail knocked over, and 15 points are scored if all fall at one shot.

Button Snap:

Lanes about a foot wide are marked along the floor, and each player is supplied with two buttons. One he places on the starting line. With the other he snaps the first one down his lane to the goal as soon as the signal is given. Snapping consists in pressing the edge of one button with the other in such a way that the under one flies ahead. If a button leaves its lane it must be put back at the line and start again. Obstacles over which the buttons must go add interest to the game. The player who first drives his button to the goal wins the game.

Match Darts:

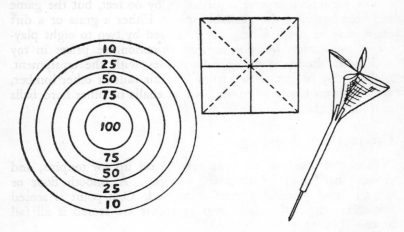

Three darts are made by cutting the heads from matches, slitting one end so that a piece of folded paper about 2½ inches square can be slipped in, and forcing into the other end the head of a large sewing needle. A target whose outside circle is not more than 15 inches in diameter is drawn on a wall board and hung shoulder high on the wall. The players stand about 8 feet away from the target, and each tries to throw the three darts so as to pierce the target as near the bullseye as he can. For each dart that sticks firmly in a space the player receives the number of points marked in that space. Nothing is counted for darts touching a line.

The accompanying illustrations show how the darts and targets should be made.

CHAPTER TEN

Choral Speaking

Because Choral Speaking is becoming very popular in schools, universities, churches, and in some sections of the country, a brief explanation and description in its simpler form is here given. For a more detailed study the reader is referred to the books listed in the Appendix under *Choral Speaking*.

The author makes no claim for originality of comments or ideas which follow. They are based upon sources placed at his disposal by a friend.

What Choral Speaking Is:

Choral Speaking is the resurrection of an art used in the Greek dramas as early as 500 B. C., and by small groups in China as early as 200 A. D. It is concert work which encourages confidence in the timid, cooperativeness in the individualistic, and self-expression in the entire group. Public schools are teaching it because it has universal appeal, and age, race and nationality present no barriers to the enjoyment of this recreation.

Poetry, and often prose, is not read well. Choral Speaking tends to stimulate diction through clear-cut pronunciation, enunciation and articulation; voice control from correct breathing to flexibility of range and tone; ear training from movement to the mood of the words.

This activity is not a sing-song repeating of poems or prose, but the bringing out of the best that is in each selection of literature used. While experimentation is necessary with anything new, the teacher or person using this recreation should give it only such time and attention as seems reasonable and commensurate with other equally important activities.

Directions for Conducting:

Select and type, or mimeograph, simple rhythmic selections with a chorus. Pass out the typed or mimeographed sheets to the participants. Allot parts to each person according to individual voice quality, and begin.

EXAMPLE (1)

(For children from 6 to 12 years of age.)

*The Song of the Pop-corn:

Type: Line-A-Child, *with* Refrain

UNISON. "Pop-pop-pop!"
1ST CHILD. Says the pop-corn in the pan;
UNISON. "Pop-pop-pop!
2ND CHILD. You may catch me if you can!"

UNISON. "Pop-pop-pop!"
3RD CHILD. Says each kernel, hard and yellow;
UNISON. "Pop-pop-pop!
4TH CHILD. I'm a dancing little fellow!"

UNISON. "Pop-pop-pop!
5TH CHILD. How I scamper through the heat!"
UNISON. "Pop-pop-pop!
6TH CHILD. You will find me good to eat."

UNISON. "Pop-pop-pop!
7TH CHILD. I can whirl and skip and hop!"
UNISON. Pop-pop-pop-pop!

Pop!

Pop!

Pop!

—Louise Abney

*Used by permission of Expression Company, Boston, Mass., from the book, "Choral Speaking Arrangement for the Upper Grades," by Louise Abney and Grace Rowe.

*The Bugle Song:

EXAMPLE (2)

(To be used for older groups. Type: Refrain)

SOLO.

> The splendor falls on castle walls
>   And snowy summits old in story;
> The long light shakes across the lakes,
>   And the wild cataract leaps in glory.

REFRAIN.

> Blow, bugle, blow; set the wild echoes flying:
> Blow, bugle; answer, echoes, dying, dying, dying.

SOLO.

> O Hark! O hear! how thin and clear,
>   And thinner, clearer, farther going!
> O sweet and far, from cliff and scar,
>   The horns of Elfland faintly blowing!

REFRAIN.

> Blow, let us hear the purple glens replying:
> Blow, bugle; answer, echoes, dying, dying, dying.

SOLO.

> O love, they die in yon rich sky,
>   They faint on hill, or field, or river.
> Our echoes roll from soul to soul,
>   And grow forever and forever.

REFRAIN.

> Blow, bugle, blow; set the wild echoes flying,
> And answer, echoes, answer, dying, dying, dying.

—*Alfred Lord Tennyson*

NOTE: A bugle sounding taps may be effectively used as a musical prelude to this selection

---

*Used by permission of the Expression Company, Boston, Mass., from the book mentioned on the preceding page. This selection taken from page 65 of that book.

CHAPTER ELEVEN

Suggestions for Party Costumes

The purpose of these sketches is to provide a study for assembling costumes for parties and masquerades.

Note:

By using inexpensive materials, as cambric, cheese cloth, etc., costumes may be made at a minimum cost. White bristol board may be used for starched collars or cuffs. In some cases crepe paper may be used for costumes or trimming very effectively.

Hats and buckles may be made of cardboard.

NATIONALITY COSTUMES

TYPICAL PEASANT COSTUME

DUTCH GIRL

DUTCH BOY

SPANISH

BAVARIAN OR ALPINE COSTUME

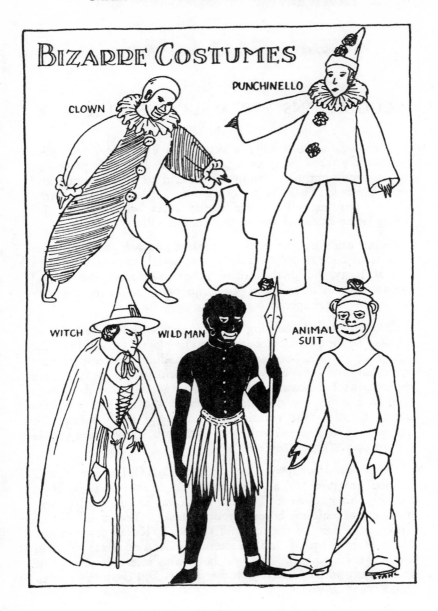

CHAPTER TWELVE

SUGGESTIONS FOR A SUCCESSFUL PARTY

A few games hurriedly. selected and executed may suffice occasionally for a party or a play period. But such procedure can not long endure. Group fun should be well planned and well directed. There is no other way for a successful party. These brief suggestions are actual rules which every play leader or recreational committee should follow carefully.

First, decide upon the kind of party you are going to have. If it is to be seasonal, patriotic, pre-nuptial, or any kind of a special party, build the entire program around the central theme. Obtain ideas from game and party books in your city library for these special occasions.

Second, detailed planning and preparation should be made in advance of the party. Select games to be played according to the age group and kind of party. Strike a medium between the very strenuous and less active games. Even young people have the capacity for becoming tired or losing interest if the games tend to lean in one direction, either to the too active or too quiet. Equalize the running and sitting games. Where the group is mixed, even with very little tots, have some games all can play. *Neglect no one.*

Third, know what you are going to do. Unless you have a definite program and a clear conception of every activity from the beginning to the end of the program, be prepared to witness severe criticism beyond your hearing. To have a list of games on a sheet of paper is not sufficient. Know those games. Have each in mind and so definitely learned that you will know every detail, and you will be able to interpret each game so concisely and so clearly that the players will definitely understand what to do.

Fourth, avoid ambiguous speech. While you may have a very clear conception of your vocabulary, there are those in the average party who can understand only simple words. Use simple language to explain each game. Never sacrifice the fun of others to impress individual importance. Be the servant of the group.

Fifth, ignore no one. The hesitant and late-comers, old people and children, regardless of age, like to play. Endeavor to make each person feel important to the success of the play period. The aged and small children are sensitive to neglect. Permit no one to go home with an injured feeling. Neither tire an individual by coaxing or pleading.

Sixth, avoid monotony. Stop the game and begin another when the players are enjoying it the most.

*Seventh, when necessary provide prizes. But do not practice giving rewards. *Play should be enjoyed for the fun of it, and not for the pay of it.* Cooperative endeavor without continuous material reward makes for more wholesome living.

Eighth, if you are a standing game leader serving for a period of time, digest the above principles entotal so that you need not refer to them often, but will have them written in your mind.

Ninth, leave nothing to chance. Have all materials for the party and each game arranged in advance.

"A One-Sided Party"

This is a clever party when plans have been carefully made to carry it out. The invitations should be prepared in an original manner, as for instance, a sketch of one side of a green tree on a white cardboard of about the size of a postcard. It might be a St. Patrick's Day party, keeping the green color all through the arrangements, as desired.

INVITATIONS: In green ink, print the words on the card:
> "Come with a smile and something green,
> Bring lots of pep, and a sweet colleen;
> Wear a gown with one side all awry,
> So we'll think you're a tough, one-sided guy;
> Come early and stay as long as you wish,
> And bring a one-sided covered dish."

PARTNERS: Cut up into two pieces, large-sized shamrocks made of green cardboard. On one side of each piece write part of an Irish name such as "Mur" on one piece, and "phy" on the other piece, making a pair, or partners for the evening. Hide these pieces round the rooms and have the guests hunt for them as soon as they arrive. The hunt and the funny costumes of the guests will start things off with a bang as the pieces are found, matched, and the guests partnered. Since the chairs have been arranged in twos, the guests will find seating arrangements easily.

DECORATIONS: The decorations for this party should be be green boughs of laurel or rhodendron, spruce, hemlock, growing shrubs, green paper bells and artificial snakes, and other novelties.

QUESTION GAME: Prepare carefully ten questions about Ireland, not too difficult, of course, and one or two funny ones.

1. Is Irish moss Irish?
2. What is a Hibernian?
3. Who is St. Patrick?

4.   Which would you rather kiss the Blarney Stone, or a girl?

5.   Of what ocean is the Irish Sea a part?

6.   Is the Irish Free State self-governing?

7.   Do you believe there are any snakes in Ireland? Tell story briefly.

8.   Did you ever see a one-sided Irish spud?

9.   What is the speech of Ireland called?

10.   What is the capital of the Irish Free State?

Number cards up to ten, attach green cord and pencil, and give the cards only to the men, rather one-sided, you see. The men will have to do all the work, and the women get the prizes. Prizes should be green baskets filled with all kinds of green things, candy in green paper, olives, green lollypops, mint candies, little cakes with green icing, a cabbage, head of lettuce, and similar suggestions, all in the spirit of fun. Consolation prizes might be large spools of green lingerie ribbon.

FISHING GAME: After this question game, something lively is in order, so invite the guests to go fishing for snakes! In a deep box have articles that are long like shoe strings, handkerchiefs rolled long, thin, big pencils, magazines rolled long and thin. Attach pin to a line and pole and ask the guests to try and "Pull the snakes out of Ireland". Prizes for this stunt may be omitted, of course, as the fun is in the landing of a wrapped prize. There may be a time limit.

REFRESHMENTS: Since the guests were invited to bring a one-sided covered dish, the refreshments may take the form of a covered dish luncheon. This would most assuredly be full of merriment as the guests would doubtless put many a surprise in their one-sided covered dishes. If preferred, the hostess may prepare her own refreshments, serving from either dining room table, buffet, or from trays in the lap, or on small tables. Have the service green in every possible way, trays, green glass dishes, green carnations or shamrocks for favors or on napkins.

MENU: Sandwiches filled with cream cheese containing bits of green gum drops. Lettuce salad, with mashed potato and parsley chopped together and mixed with mayonnaise until creamy. Drop in light spoonsful on lettuce leaf and sprinkle chopped citron around them. Saltines. Brick ice cream with shamrock in green on top of the brick. Sunshine and Angel Food cake. Green candies. Coffee. This menu may be simplified as desired. The idea of one-sidedness should be carried out in the menu by cutting corners off the sandwiches, salad on one side of the plate only, ice cream bricks crosswise on plate, cakes iced or cut in odd shapes, green candies in one half side of dish. Guests should be asked to drink their coffee from one side of cup. If guests join wholeheartedly in the fun and are present with one side of the face rouged, the other without make-up; one side of hair done high, the other low; men with neckties to one side, success is sure to follow.

"An Indian Masquerade Party"

All people delight in reading about the Indians of long ago. A party carrying out the ideas and customs of the Indians would be quite effective and unusual. This party might be given in a home and prove very enjoyable, or in a large hall or assembly room, and be a semester party, when there is a breathing space between semesters—and work!

INVITATIONS: Select yellow cards for the invitations, and print or write on them in black letters as follows:
"You are cordially invited to smoke a pipe of peace with us, at the home of Miss Edna Stapleton, Marsh Road, on Saturday evening, January third, at eight-o'clock. Be a Brave, a Squaw, a Papoose, or a Medicine man but be sure and come in costume, and masked."
Sketch a pipe of peace on the cards, and be sure and add the smoke! Or a tepee drawn upon the cards would be correct.

DECORATIONS: These should consist, even if the party is to be in a home, of all the Indian ideas possible, a tepee, totem pole, trees, branches, sweet grass baskets, blankets, rugs, relics that tell a real story, pictures of famous Indian chiefs. No real Indian party would ever be complete without the Indian's own tribal symbols; it would be hardly possible to overdo it.

PARTNERS: Prepare bright-colored arrows. On one write a conundrum, on another, the answer to it. Hide these arrows all around the rooms or hall. Guests are to locate them and pair off by mating up the riddles correctly.

HUNTING THE GAUNTLET GAME: While still masked, if possible, and partnered by the arrows, invite the guests to run the gauntlet by walking two pieces of tape that have been stretched from one side of the room to another side, having a girl at one tape and a boy at the other tape. At a given signal, the game is to carry successfully on a silver knife, as many beads as possible (medium-sized beads all alike) from one side of the room to the other without once stepping off from the rope. To make it more like running the gauntlet, guests might be permitted mild comments to disconcert the players. The partners carrying the most beads to the goal are declared winners of the game. Each couple has a chance, and the prize should be a beaded bag or a pair of moccasins or an Indian story book which both girl and boy could read.

DIVERSIONS: Story of Pocohontas acted in tableau form.
Indian dances, ceremonials, by groups.
Peace pipe smoking by tribes, or groups.
Indian songs.
Indian instrumentals.

REFRESHMENTS: Indirect lighting for the party, typifying dusk or evening. Guests seated round a fireplace on floor for refreshments. Serve salad in large bowl with wooden spoon, guests to help themselves, on wooden plates. Pass small crackers, nuts, candies in baskets, and small glasses of punch that will set upon the wooden plates without trouble or upset. Guests unmask during refreshments, or at any previous time the host or hostess may choose.

"An Indoor Beach Party"

This party is best carried out where there is a large hall or assembly room, but it may be adapted to a home entertainment by carrying it out on a smaller scale. A real beach party should be a riot of color and gaiety and fun.

INVITATIONS: These may be sent out in the form of fancy beach postcards of regular size, or upon miniature beach postcards which come twelve in a package for about ten cents. In both cases envelopes would have to be bought separately. If preferred, correspondence cards and their envelopes may be used, buying several colors, and pasting on the cards any beach scenes you may find, or painting a sketch in one corner with water colors. Beach snapshots might also be used.

"An indoor beach party will be held at the home of Arabella Wilson, Fifteen East End Boulevard, on Saturday, December ninth, at eight-thirty o'clock. Come in beach togs, bathing suits crossed off! Fun and frolic."

If the party is to be on a large scale, the class artist might design invitations in the shape of sea shells, and paint or draw upon them beach sketches in colors.

DECORATIONS: Secure several of the gay beach umbrellas to be used in the corners of the hall over tables where refreshments are to be served during the evening. Beach chairs may be used also but as they take up much room, one or two would be enough. Folding small chairs may always be rented at small cost. Gay bunting, flags, blankets, posters all add to the effect and are not difficult to obtain.

THE GEOGRAPHICAL GAME: Form the guests in two long lines, standing, down the hall. A bright, snappy leader acts as referee. The game is to name a city or town beginning with "A". There should be a reasonable time limit, yet the game should move swiftly as a whole. One side calls out name of city beginning with "A". The other side follows suit as quickly as possible, and so on, down the two lines. If a player cannot think of a name, he goes over to the other side. In this game it is easy enough at the beginning but the "A" names soon begin to come harder and players get "stuck". Referee may change letters when the game moves too slowly to be interesting. This game which may be played seated, if desired, calls for quick thinking and some geographical knowledge. Many a queer name pops up!

WALKING THE TIGHT ROPE: Stretch a rope across the room or hall, tightly and securely. Invite the guests to walk this rope without once stepping off, carrying a bright gay, parasol at the same time over and back to the starting place. This may be varied by asking players to open and close the parasol on the trip. Prizes for this game should be given to the girl who does it correctly and most gracefully and to the man who does it correctly and in the most dignified manner. The consolation prize should be awarded to the funniest performer who at the same time does it correctly. Prizes should take the form of bathing bags, suntan suits, beach hats, and a tin pail and shovel for the consolation prize.

DIVERSIONS: There may be a few diversions such as shooting at bobbing heads, swinging balloons, fortune-telling stands, games of chance, and stunts that may be used as fillers.

REFRESHMENTS: During the evening refreshments should be served from the umbrella stands in small tin beach pails. Punch, fancy cakes, nuts and candy are suitable for this. If more elaborate refreshments are desired there is a novel idea of inviting the guests to partake of them while marching by the stands, or even while running. This could be at the close of the party. From the first booth "beach sand-wiches" are handed out quickly, made of one slice of white bread and one slice of dark, with different fillings. From the next booth, or stand, the second time around, a large olive (stuffed) run through with a toothpick, is served and the third time around, slowly, an ice cream cone, guests to find comfortable seats, and listen to a few sailor songs and tunes.

"A Romany Rendezvous"

A delightful party may be carried out in a small grove of trees, not too far from home or highway. This should take the form of a Gypsy party and is suitable for a large or small number of guests. If the weather is unfavorable, it may be carried out in the house, with small change of plans.

INVITATIONS: The invitations should be written or printed on cards on which a black Gypsy kettle has been neatly pasted or painted, with a few reddish flames for effect. The words which follow may be used on the cards:

"Romany Rendezvous in the grove near the home of Will Johnson, five Cedar Avenue, on Friday evening, at eight-thirty o'clock, September twentieth. You are cordially invited to come, and *commanded* to dress in Gypsy costume, or wear something which Gypsies like to wear. Or east, or west, dark night is best, to carry out our chief's behest."

DECORATIONS: The grove is to be lighted with lanterns, the common barn variety is better than fancy Japanese, or with electric lights if this is possible. Chairs, rugs, cushions, small tables are placed around, here and there, and if unfavorable weather is feared, an awning may be arranged and chairs and other decorative furniture, placed beneath it. A stone fireplace should be built in a safe spot for a good rousing camp fire, and this should be lighted at a late hour. Have at least one big black Gypsy kettle swinging from forked sticks. The grove may be reached by hiking or automobile in September, before the leaves are off the trees, and at a time when it is most difficult to give up the vacation days outdoors. September is also an ideal month for an indoor Romany Rendezvous, since it may serve as a friendly get-together for the long school months.

DIVERSIONS: All who play musical instruments should take them along as Gypsy music is full of thrills. All who can sing should work up a few Gypsy songs, in the spirit of cooperation. The girls dress in gay colors, bangles, kerchiefs, shawls, or bands of ribbon; the boys with gay neckties, handkerchiefs, scarfs, odd hats and shoes, and fancy vests. The host or hostess dresses as a Gypsy chieftain, or queen and welcomes the guests in the grove which should be lighted at first.

PARTNERS: The first name of each guest is printed in large letters and pinned to the backs with clasp pins so they will not fall off. A tin dish on a table holds the first names of the girls. The boys are given one printed name, or draw a name for themselves, and are told to hunt for partners "Catherine", "Doris" and so forth. When there are two or more names alike in a large group, mark the cards "Catherine the First", "Catherine the Third", to avoid confusion. After the guests have paired off, it is time for a fortune hunt.

FORTUNE HUNT: Prepare beforehand a fortune for each guest on circles of cardboard and conceal a fortune for a boy and girl, together, in some spot behind a tree, under leaves, tied to a branch, in a clump of bushes, buried in the ground with two sticks carelessly crosses on top, under a rock, and so forth. The guests in pairs hunt their fortunes together and read them when found. Write the fortunes in a jolly way, as follows:
"Your husband will be head of a great college, be bald, wear spectacles, be very generous, but not inclined to go to parties. You have already met him, but will meet him again under a romantic moon."

*   *   *

"Your wife will be handsome, loving, easy to manage, and very wealthy, but she will have a roving disposition, and keep you always in a panic as to her where-abouts. She will be a blonde."

The next game is with the guests seated with paper and pencils, endeavoring to get the most words out of "Romany Rendezvous" in fifteen minutes time. The first prize may be a gay silk scarf for the girl with the highest score and a similar scarf or muffler for the top boy. The consolation prize may be a bright-colored handkerchief filled with peanuts.

The next game should be a lively one like Puss-in-the-Corner, using the trees for corners. Or an obstacle race may be in order.

OBSTACLE RACE: Tie a white rope or tape to various trees in a sort of path or track. Invite each guest to travel along the path at a slow trot, pick up the various obstacles along the way, and convey them intact to the starting point. These obstacles should be difficult to pick up, like wet soap, a slippery tool, a straw, a piece of rubber and so forth. If this promises to take too long, ask the guests to pick up the article and put it back again, and his time will be recorded by a timekeeper. One who makes the race in the best time may be awarded a prize of a gay Gypsy handkerchief.

REFRESHMENTS: These should consist of sandwiches served from a shiny new skillet in which a paper doily may be placed; several kinds of cookies and small cakes served from a Gypsy sweet grass basket; soft drinks and coffee. Seat the guests around the campfire and start Gypsy tales while all are enjoying the refreshments. A good story teller can put a delightful finishing touch to a Romany Rendezvous. This is the time, also, to have the guests who can play or sing gay songs, use their talents to their best ability, and if small souvenirs of sweet grass novelties may be given the guests as mementoes of the party, there wil surely be many happy memories of the Romany Rendez-vous.

"Comic Valentine Party"

This is a variation of the usual Valentine party, and will prove highly amusing and delightful. No one particularly enjoys the comic valentine which is close to offensiveness but there are many comic valentine ideas that are just full of agreable fun and humor, so do try a Comic Valentine party, just for a change, and the results will surely prove a pleasant surprise.

INVITATIONS: Invitations to guests should be comic valentines, really clever, funny ones, with a good verse. Each invitation may have a head cut from a magazine pasted on, and tinted with water colors, rather than a comic figure already on most valentines, with the verse. The comic verse counts most, with original touches added. The wording on the back or inside of the valentine should be as follows:

"Would like to have you come to my Comic Valentine Party, on Friday evening, at eight-thirty o'clock, February twelfth. If you have an old-fashioned rig you can don, it would be great fun. Home of Esther Waters, Boulevard Avenue, Clifton Township."

DECORATIONS: These may be oddities, funny pictures from magazines, people in funny poses, comic arrangement of flowers in vases, chairs in unusual positions, various objects in places where they should not be, the general idea being to produce a comic effect around the rooms and create laughs galore. In a hall, use comic draperies, cushions, and arrangement of furniture.

PARTNERS: To pair off the guests for this party, cut comic valentines in half and number each part the same, number one on both pieces, number two, and so forth, until you have as many as you have guests. Invite the young people to hunt for their "better halves". It will take some scrambling to locate the various pieces and match them up correctly. After the halves have been made "one", the first game is in order, and is entirely in the spirit of fun for couples.

MISSOURI GAME: Line up the partners for this game, facing each other, but about two or three feet between the lines, so that the exhibitions may be readily seen by all. The idea is that each player wants to be "shown", so when the leader says "Partners number one, girl show the man how she would propose to him!"—the girl player acts out her proposal as seriously as she can, going up to him, and kneeling, or otherwise making it very realistic, by actions and words. The man will be somewhat embarrassed but "game". The two lines of players enjoy the fun. Next, the man must show his partner how he would accept such a proposal. And so on, down the lines, the leader gives to each couple a clever question and answer which they must act out.

"How would you eat spaghetti?"

"How would you give your pet dog a bath?"

As soon as this game is finished, and the guests have all become seated, try the next stunt, which is a test of skill in sewing and fashioning a doll that will look lifelike.

RAG DOLL SEWING BEE: Give to each guest one-half yard of plain, bright-colored cloth, like gingham, or print. Also, soft pencils, and needles and thread and pins. The object is to see who can fashion the best rag doll with the material and tools, using the pencils to draw the faces on the cloth after the doll is made. Most likely, this sewing bee will result in a few more comic valentine dolls, and the fun will be continuous. The best doll made by a man receives a prize of a book of comic stories, or humorous fiction; the best by a girl a prize of fancy hose in very gay color or design. There should be a fair time limit for this sewing bee as men are rather slow with needles. Newspaper, tissue paper, cotton batten, etc., may be used also.

DIVERSIONS: A huge paper comic figure is hung on the wall. Guests are to fill in hair, eyes, nose, and so forth with crayons, or soft pencils. One dish soapy water; one dish clear water; one empty dish. Blindfolded girls test their fortune by putting hands into a dish, if they can, the first prophecying an "early widow"; the second a "happy marriage"; the third a "spinster".

REFRESHMENTS: Candy in odd shapes; crackers stuck together; sandwiches very large and very tiny, and in odd shapes; cake with several colors of icing in designs; cookies in doll-like shapes made by some bakery; salad and ice cream in dishes all different as to shape and color; napkins with comic pictures. Partners should change during sewing bee and refreshments.

"A Chinese Party"

This kind of a party gives ample opportunity for ingenuity and variety. China is a country of strange customs, strange dress and strange manners—that is, strange to us because we were not born Orientals. It is surely a delight to pass an evening in an Oriental atmosphere of fun and frolic, and a Chinese party should please all young people, and prove delightfully different.

INVITATIONS: These should be on very thin white or rice paper, and in one corner paste or paint a band of light reddish color similar to laundry checks and draw Chinese characters in black in columns upon it, or a good imitation of same. The wording of the invitations may be something like this:

"Miss Bertha James is giving a Chinese party at her home, Saturday evening, April tenth, at eight-thirty o'clock, and cordially invites you to be present. Would like to have you wear some object representative of China for a game."

The invitations may also be in the form of a black dragon cut from heavy paper, and the wording done in white ink. Envelopes should be white, or black and white combined.

DECORATIONS: China is a country of mystery and charm, and that should be the key note of the decorative scheme. For a home party, the rooms should be well filled with bowls and vases of flowers, either real or artificial, growing lilies and ferns. Large black dragons cut from paper may be fastened to walls. Chinese lanterns should be used whenever safe, with no danger of fire. Long streamers of pink paper with large black Chinese characters in columns upon them should be fastened here and there. Chinese characters are read from top to bottom. A Chinese rug or two, rattan or porch chairs, burning incense in odd-shaped receptacles typical of the East, a Buddha reposing in a conspicuous place, Chinese lilies in pretty bowls, Chinese pictures or prints, lovely silk shawls or scarfs prominently displayed—all of these suggestions add to the Oriental decorative scheme. In a hall or assembly room, a typical Chinese scene may be arranged along one side of the room—a sampan, rickshaw, and other Chinese objects, as far as may be procured or constructed in amateur fashion, one or two booths with display of Chinese products such as china dishes, tea, rice, trinkets made in China, and perhaps weird music in one booth of the Chinese variety produced by a victrola or a group of musicians. One or more of these ideas may be used according to need, space, expense, and availability. The colors of the Chinese flag—crimson, yellow, blue, white and black—may be used in combination with striking effect in bunting or crepe paper, or in large painted bands on white. For a small party, it would not take very long to make a few flags from these colors of cloth, and display them well. A Chinese party whether in a hall or in a private home must have the intriguing touches of the Orient with mysterious corners, draperies arranged as if concealing something, dim lights, faint perfumes or incense, stealthy footsteps and low voices.

GAME:—"CHINESE GUESSING GAME"

The first game should be the guessing of the names of the Chinese objects worn or represented by the guests. These may be paper, tea, cotton, mulberry plant picture, bamboo cane, opium pipe, picture of a bird's nest, fan, embroidery, porcelain, emperor, Buddha rice, picture of boy "peeking", Manchuria, and others equally as good. If any of the guests come in Chinese costume, or wearing a Mandarin coat, so much the better for realism. Prizes for guessing correctly the most Chinese names represented may be a Chinese teapot, decorative package of tea, or quaint Chinese print or vase which may be purchased at a good art store. First prize for the men might be a silk scarf.

DIVERSIONS: Guessing the number of grains of rice in a glass jar. Tossing tea balls at a suspended basket for mock basket ball. A Chinese film run backwards which would create fun. Each guest describe one Chinese custom, person, or place.

GAME:—"PASS THE QUARTER"

Whether the guests "pass the quarter" exams or not, all can play at it, and have a good deal of fun. Have the guests sit upon the floor Chinese fashion, in a close circle. The leader of this game shakes hands with all the guests, and in one palm he leaves a quarter in American money. The guests try to shake hands with each other, and talk "velley muchee likee Chinaman" to divert attention, and whoever has the quarter must get it into another palm without being detected. A person who is "it" tries to locate the quarter; if he does, he is out of the game, but he gives the quarter to the leader who starts it round again. This game must move fairly fast to be the most fun, and the actions of the guesser and the guests will provide plenty of laughs and guilty looks. If it is not possible or desirable to have the guests sit on the floor, they may be seated closely around a table to play this game. If a piece of Chinese money is available, use it.

GAME:—"PINNING THE EYE ON THE CHINAMAN"

In this game which is a laugh-provoker, the committee or hostess should make a large Chinese face of yellow muslin or print cloth. Make features out of black cloth and stitch on to the yellow face, all except one eye. Let the guests give the Chinaman "a black eye" and mirth will reign supreme, for it is not easy to do. Blindfold one guest, give him the black eye with a pin run through it, turn him round once, and head him very direct toward the Chinaman's face. If the guest is a steady walker and does not get excited or nervous, he may pin the eye where it belongs, but if the player feels the loss of both his own good eyes, he may pin the Chinaman's eye almost anywhere, from his pigtail to his left ear, and the result will be ludicrous enough. If the black eyes are made almond-shaped, and a pig tail shows just a little, the effect will be quite Oriental and funny. The high-class Chinese are very modern in appearance, well educated, and splendid people to meet, but for the purpose of this little game, we may call the Chinaman one of the type we find in any country, just a native.

GAME:—"FLYING TO CHINATOWN"

At one end of the room, or hall, arrange two goals about four feet apart. They may be designed to form a gateway and arch on which the word "Chinatown" is printed in large letters. The players stand on a tape, and back about eight or ten feet or more from the goal, two players at a time. Each is given a pasteboard fan with the word "Chinatown" on it along with a small black and white sketch of China or Chinatown. These fans may be gotten up in artistic manner, and used as souvenirs of the party, presented to the guests after this game. Out of different colors of tissue paper, make butterflies rather small, and with wings that will blow good. The two players try to see who can "fly to Chinatown" first, by blowing the paper butterflies with their fans inside the goals. Sometimes an elastic band around a piece of tissue paper makes a splendid butterfly. Make the butterflies all colors. Have a time limit if the players are not speedy enough. Give just a small firt prize, a ten-cent *china* dish, to each winner, or to the player who does it in the best time. Give the fans also to all the players. Make these stiff enough to withstand use reasonably well, for the game may wax furious. In a home, ordinary books piled up, may constitute the two goals, and the paper may be rolled into balls instead of fancy butterflies, and plain palm leaf fans may be used. It sounds easy enough, but like *any* well-regulated butterfly, the pieces of tissue paper will cause many a wild goose chase.

REFRESHMENTS: These should, of course, consist of tea served in several delightful ways, with servers in costume if possible. Costumes need not be out of the question since a white middy blouse over pajama trousers, peaked hat, and so forth, would do very well indeed. Refreshments may be served to guests seated on low chairs or cushions, or rugs, or at a large table with a China Pagoda for a center-piece, made out of childrens' blocks, the better grade, of course. A pagoda is a towerlike storied structure, usually a temple, or a memorial and is used in India, China, and Japan, the word probably coming from the noun "pagod" meaning an idol.

Dainty buttered rolls on lovely chinaware; several relishes in a fancy dish: thin slices of meat on Chinese trays; rice pudding in molds; nuts and preserved Canton ginger; this is one menu suitable for a Chinese party. China dishes only should be used, and pretty napkins covered with gay flowers add to the enjoyment of the refreshments. During the serving have a good story-teller relate a trip through Chinatown in New York. Other guests, who have visited these Chinese quarters, contributing items of weird interest.

China is really a wonderful country, from its great wall to its smallest bit of pottery, and a Chinese party should be just the ways of the Chinese re-enacted, bit by bit, with the suave, extremely-polite manners of the race adding much to the educational interest of such a party and making it realistic.

"A Christmas Joy-Party"

No time of the year is so lovely for a party! No time of the year is so full of joy, good cheer, and consideration for others! Did you ever look at the word "Christmas" and see why it is so full of joy? It has charm in it, and the Christ who gave us Christmas, and although a Christmas party may be as wild and free as one chooses to make it, yet there will always creep in, just a bit of the real spirit of the holiday, and a little of its solemn meaning.

INVITATIONS: These should be festive in every way, and there are so many lovely Christmas cards with envelopes that it might be more practical to buy these instead of making original ones. For those who take pleasure in preparing original invitations, select a light green card and envelope to match. In the ten-cent stores one may find Christmas seals in black and silver, and these may be used on the cards. Around the seal, paint in dark green, a wreath as best you can, or a plain band, with red bow from the bottom of it. Then write the following words:

> Christmas joy is not complete,
> Unless we all together meet,
> So to my home just wend your way,
> And Yuletide joy shall have full sway.

Martha Wilson   Ten Front Street
Eight o'clock   R.S.V.P.
December   Twentieth

Place a small seal or Santa Claus in the corner of envelope.

DECORATIONS: It hardly seems necessary to specify these, because there is nothing so effective as artistic evergreens with red touches here and there, but for a change one might try having all the decorations in red and silver.

Silver tinsel, streamers of silver paper, Christmas letters in silver. A Santa Claus in huge silver robe and setting, with a touch of red on his face, cap, and mittens, silver bells, red bells, paint thorn apple branches, or any other branches from trees with alumnium paint, and fasten red cranberries on the thorns. In a hall, have the decorations striking rather than too elaborate, perhaps mostly in the corners, leaving the sides free for chairs, and a huge Santa Claus in some alcove. In a home, keep the decorations very artistic, baskets of silver leaves and red berries or poinsettias, a few bowls of red poinsettias on the tables on silver mats, and a few silver vases with red flowers.

GAME:—"WHO'S WHO IN SANTA CLAUS LAND?"

Prepare lists of propensities of the guests beforehand, one list for each guest, as follows:
1. Who is the best caroller in the room?
2. Who has the biggest "Sweet Tooth"?
3. Who likes the boys the best?
4. Who has the best Christmas smile?
5. Who studies the hardest just before Christmas?
6. Who is the best ball player?
7. Who is the best dancer?
8. Who is the best pal?
9. Who has the most expressive eyes?
10. Who is the squarest shooter?

The game is to answer these questions, each guest writing the answers on the tally provided. The tallies are collected and the person receiving the most votes on each question is the winner announced. Mary Jones receives the most votes as the best caroller, and she is invited to give an exhibition. Each winner is asked to illustrate the propensity in which she comes out a winner, the results being funny and clever.

GAME:—"SANTA CLAUS CHAIR"

Arrange one less number of chairs in a circle, or letter "C" (for Christmas) than you have players. A person at the piano plays Christmas songs and stops suddenly! All the players try to get seated instantly, but some one will be left out, and he is Santa Claus and must wear a jingling bell on a red band around his neck. The music begins again and Santa Claus tries hard to get a chair, and if he does, some other person must put on the bell and play the game. This game moves quickly, is lots of fun, and may continue as long as the players wish. Or one chair may be taken away each time, and the game limited.

DIVERSIONS: Talk fast one minute. Imitate peddler. Imitate Christmas radio announcer. Imitate turkey gobbling, sleigh bells, dog barking, sing part of favorite song or carol, recite two lines of Christmas poem, say "I love you" loud, and then very soft. Blow out candle, either in one blow, or at greatest distance. Use a red candle in a silver candlestick. Blindfold for this.

GAME:—"CHRISTMAS TELETYPE MESSAGES"

Mix up letters of a Christmas word such as "Yuletide" in a large envelope. Other words may be "Carolling", "Mistletoe", "ornaments", "Santa Claus", "evergreens", and so forth, words being of about the same length for fairness. Allow a short time for getting the letters together to form the word in each envelope, the first person to call out "I have mine" to receive ten pennies, for a prize, the second person nine pennies, and so on down to one penny for the slowest.

GAME:—"INITIAL LIFE STORIES"

While the guests are still seated, pass papers and let each guest write upon his paper the initials of the person on his right, and turn down the paper, passing it on to the next. The leader asks clever questions such as: "How old are you"?, "Where were you born?", "How much do you weigh?", "Were you ever in love?" and so forth. Answers are written as each paper is passed. The person claiming the initials reads as follows, his life story.

"I am as old as Methuselah. Was born in Picardy. Weigh about two tons. I was in love at sixteen with a travelling salesman. He turned me down."

Most of the life stories will not be suitable for publication.

GAME:—"PINNING THE HEAD ON A TURKEY"

For a little moving around, have the guests pin a head on a gaily-feathered turkey on a sheet. First prize, a huge candy cane for a man, a candy Santa Claus for a girl player.

GAME:—"BIRDS' CHRISTMAS CAROL"

Cut up a typewritten copy of this lovely Christmas story into about as many parts as you expect guests. Number and distribute the parts and ask guests to read in order of numbers, quite rapidly, so that the story will move along more swiftly and interestingly. This keeps the guests seated for some time and it is well to serve the refreshments in some novel way to provide an opportunity for moving about a little.

REFRESHMENTS: Serve the refreshments at small tables, and place two ladies at each table to act as hostesses. The idea is for the men to visit the tables for two minutes or so, and enjoy fruit cocktails at the first table. A bell is rung and the men progress to another table for a five-minute visit and delicious sandwiches of all kinds and pickles also at this table. The sandwiches and pickles may be brought in and served from the small tables in silver dishes, or fancy colored dishes, after the first course of cocktails has been removed. The men next progress to the last table course which is ice cream and cake, and coffee, or one more change of tables may be made, and coffee, nuts and candy served at the last one. Small tables may be beautifully arranged for a Christmas Joy-Party, using very lovely lunch cloths and napkins, centerpiece of two corsage bouquets of silver and red, and these to be given to the two hostesses when the party is over. If expense must be considered, provide crepe paper luncheon sets which are most lovely nowadays, and artificial flower corsages. If possible, use all one-colored glass dishes for serving, or silver and red dishes. The men may be given small boxes of Christmas candies for souvenirs.

"A Good Neighbor Party"

There is an old saying "good fences make good neighbors", and in a great many ways this adage is true, for fences keep one neighbor from encroaching upon another's rights; they keep peace; they settle all boundary lines; they inspire respect and real friendship. At a "Good Neighbor" party, however, there are no fences except kindness, thoughtfulness, fun without hurts, laughter without rudeness, and a good time without the least offense.

INVITATIONS: When preparing these, care should be used to make them clever as well as "neighborly". A card in the shape of a book would be a very appropriate form and the invitation written on the pages. Or a fence might be sketched on the card, and the words "Hop Over" at the top of the card. Then the usual wording below:

> Please come to my Good Neighbor party
> On Friday evening at eight o'clock
> December ninth, Fifty West Street
> Maizie George. R.S.V.P.

Good taste in invitations generally calls for white cards and envelopes, and if the party is to be a formal one, there is a formal style of wording, but for informal parties, there is more latitude. One may be original and select some dainty color scheme with sketches in ink, crayon, or water color to help carry the message. For a "Good Neighbor" party a small sketch of a "house by the side of the road" in ink, and part of the poem by the same name, would be very appropriate.

DECORATIONS: For this unusual party the decorations might be in black and white, large black bowls of white flowers; branches of thorn apple tree painted black and with white gum drops or other soft white candy stuck firmly on to the thorns; this makes a striking and novel decoration for a corner table; tall black floor baskets filled with artificial lilies especially good in a hall where there are spaces to be filled attractively. All tallies and pencils may be white with black pencils, or vice versa. Arrange the chairs in twos, to carry out the good neighbor idea and to use for the first game which is in the form of a neighborly questionnaire.

GAME:—"GOOD NEIGHBOR QUESTIONNAIRE"

In this game the guests are seated in couples. The ladies are given papers or tallies with a few words written on them, to be used as answers, such as "hot, sweet and soft", "peppery", "yes, mixed with love", "doing somersaults", and so forth. The men are to ask questions similar to the following in a loud enough voice for all to hear:

1. How do you like neighbors, Miss Jones?
2. Does your left-hand neighbor like parties?
3. How does your right-hand neighbor like books?
4. How does your neighbor go to church?

The answer that the girl player holds in her hand is read aloud, and as it may be "hot, sweet and soft" for the first question the result creates no end of merriment. After one round has been made, the answers (which have been prepared beforehand by the committee or hostess) may be collected, shuffled and passed out again. Questions may be original of course, and round two will be very different and just as funny. This game may be played as long as necessary to get everyone well into the spirit of fun, then a more lively one may be in order.

GAME:—"GUESS YOUR NEW NEIGHBOR"

In this game, players are handicapped right at the start by being blindfolded. Half of the number of guests are so blindfolded, and asked to be seated in a row of chairs, while beside each person is an empty chair for a new neighbor who is going to move in. At the ringing of a bell, the striking of a piano chord, or the blowing of a whistle, the new neighbors quietly seat themselves in the empty chairs, and each one does some little stunt by which the blindfolded guests or players attempt to guess his identity. These stunts may be soft singing, humming, mumbling, stuttering, groaning, lisping, some little trick by which they are to be named, if possible. This game requires clever acting and clever guessing, because it is astonishing how one may disguise his voice even to friends.

GAME:—"DRAW YOUR NEIGHBOR"

While guests are still seated, give out to each player, large pieces of white paper about the size of typewriting paper and soft pencils. Each player is requested to draw as well as possible, at least as recognizable as possible, a picture of his right-hand neighbor, and write the correct name on the back of the neighbor it represents. These are held up before the entire company for identification. Of course, the results are so likely to be caricatures, rather than artistic likenesses, the fun is great, but since each player is equally a "victim", neighborly toleration prevails. If any drawing merits a reward for real talent, present a small framed picture which is a professional sketch. Do not award a consolation prize as the drawing might be too much of a caricature, and break down the good neighborly fence.

GAME:—"A NEIGHBORLY RACE"

To get the guests into action a bit, try a neighborly race around the rooms or hall, using the same squares of paper on which the drawings have been made. Start the players off in couples, the idea being to lay the paper "face" up, on the floor, "step on it", lay it down again, pick it up again, and so on, around the prescribed track, one piece of paper for each foot also, if preferred, though if large pieces are used for the drawings, they would probably be large enough to stand on with both feet. It sounds much easier to do than it really is for anyone who steps off the paper, is out of the race at once. This will reduce competition pretty early in the game. There must be a reasonable time

limit for this race, and prizes of black and white handkerchiefs for all contestants who come through without any
slips.

GAME:—"BACK-FENCE GOSSIP"

All the games so far having been in the spirit of *good*
neighborliness, it seems fitting to try a bit of the other side
of the question, a gossip game. Now the idea is to say
something about one chosen member of the party, starting
the comment at one end of a circle, or a fence if you can
construct one, with all players seated. A player may volun-
teer to be the neighbor or "victim" of the gossip, then the
results cannot be taken to heart. A real back-fence comment should be started as follows: "Did you know Miss
Wilson wears a wig?" This is whispered to one's neighbor
around the circle, or over the imaginary fence, and when
the last person gets it—"perfectly straight"—of course, as
all gossip is, it sounds something like this: "Did you know
Miss Wilson's son swears like a Whig?" Miss Wilson can
gracefully "take it" of course, and is a good-natured victim.
This back-fence gossip game turns out some wonderful
news about the whole neighborhood, a lot you never knew
even about yourself. The only warning is not to select personal failings or attributes which will cause any hurt feelings.

REFRESHMENTS: A Good Neighbor party should carry
out the idea in the serving of the refreshments, and it might
be desirable to do this in cafeteria style, that is, have the
men go to the refreshment table, and get all the trays for
the ladies. In order to have the partnering go smoothly,
and without favoritism, present each lady with a black and
white badge of silk ribbon, and on each badge, a letter of
the alphabet printed artistically. If there are more guests
than letters, double up the letters, such as "A A", or even a
triple "A A A". When the men receive the trays, let each
one draw a duplicate badge from a box, and serve the lady
whose letter he draws. He selects the menu, arranges the
tray, and serves his appointed lady guest. Then the men

return, after all the ladies have been served, and procure their own trays, and eat their refreshments with their partners. This is being a good neighbor indeed, since young people are sure to favor a certain pair of eyes above all others, and wish to sit under their spell.

Refreshments for a cafeteria serving should be things easily carried or managed such as sandwiches of many kinds but cut very small; small cakes baked in paper dishes, also in many styles; small crullers sugared and plain; small squares of cheese; Brownies, a delicious confection that may be made at home; and olives and small pickles, tea and coffee and soft drinks.

"A Hallowe'en Revel"

October is a gay, festive time of the year when summer is gone, and the long wintertime full of good times indoors, friendly gatherings and class re-unions seems just a glorious interim between vacations. Studies of course will be bound to intrude, but they will not seem a troublesome asset if well-planned parties are "sandwiched" in from time to time. Hallowe'en parties are always full of mystery and shivery thrills, and are very easily gotten up and carried out.

INVITATIONS: Purchase small envelopes and a few sheets of heavy paper or cardboard. Cut cards to fit the envelopes. On one side of the card sketch with ink a section of fence with pointed boards. On the fence glue a pussy willow for the body of a cat. Pussy willows can usually be obtained at florists' shops at most any time of the year. Sketch with ink a head and long tail on the pussy willow. A moon may be added to the picture, if desired. The cats will be clever and realistic. On the other side of the card, write or print the following words:

"A Hallowe'en Revel at eight-fifteen,
Come looking your worst, but fit to be seen,
Do be sure and come, don't scowl or pout,
Or the goblins'll git yer, if yer don't watch out!
Assembly Hall   October thirty-first."

If it is not possible to obtain the pussy willows, cut a circle of black paper for the body of the cat, then add the head and tail.

DECORATIONS: These should be weird, mysterious, and the usual symbols of Hallowe'en such as huge pumpkins with faces cut in them, and a lighted candle inside; black and yellow crepe paper streamers, lattice work and huge bows here and there. Black pasteboard cats with yellow beads for eyes, and bristles for whiskers, should be placed in effective places around the hall. Black and yellow bunting may be draped over windows, around ceiling lights, doors, and so forth. As a rule, decorations for a large hall are more effective if not too profusely used. The decorative effect should be striking rather than too elaborate. It often saves time if the committee who are familiar with their hall or assembly room, get together and plan their decorations at home on paper first. By this method it might also be possible to keep the expense within treasury limits. The color orange, lends itself beautifully to Hallowe'en decorations, and if the general scheme is black and yellow, add touches of orange by means of orange crepe paper or bunting twisted into large bows, to be fastened here and there. If there is a stage or platform not needed for the revel, hem long strips of black and yellow cambric, and run it on to a rope. Attach the end of the rope at each end of the stage as high up as possible. The cloth will hang easily and hide the stage fairly well. If musicians are to be engaged for the Hallowe'en Revel, they may be seated on the stage behind the draperies, or just beneath the platform in front of the draperies as a background. All decorations in a hall should be so arranged that there is no danger from fire or accident, securely fastened in place at all points.

PARTNERS: As the guests enter the hall, give to each, tally cards in the shape of black cats, on the backs of which are lists of fifteen numbers with spaces beside them. Attach pencil and cord to each tally card, providing two only of one color, giving one set to the men, a corresponding set to the ladies. Invite the men to seek their partners by matching colors, and between them to guess the names of the "cats". If desired, the question about each cat may be on the men's tallies, the answers on the ladies' tallies. Or several sets of the questions may be printed plainly and placed in various places about the hall. The answers may be retained by some member of the committee and when the guests have all arrived and partnered, and filled in their answers on their tallies "two heads being better than one in such a game", the questions and answers may be loudly read and checked off on the tallies. The couple having the most correct answers is presented with a furry, toy cat, either black or some color. If more than one couple have correct sets of answers, they may be allowed to choose straws for the prize cat. The fifteen "cats" to be guessed and written in the spaces are these:

A CAT QUIZ

1. A cat that likes a flood ....Cataclysm
2. A cat that lives in the ground ....Catacomb
3. A cat that has fits ....Catalepsy
4. A cat that has a lot of names ....Catalogue
5. A cat that is a tree ....Catalpa
6. A cat that floats and is paddled ....Cataraman
7. A wild cat that climbs ....Catamount
8. A cat that throws stones ....Catapult
9. A cat that makes one blind ....Cataract
10. A cat that catches cold ....Catarrh
11. A cat that ends in disaster ....Catastrophe
12. A cat that is turned into wine ....Catawba
13. A cat that sings ....Catbird
14. A cat that sups ....Catsup
15. A cat that is religious ....Catechism

The above cat game is to be played only long enough to draw the guests well into the spirit of fun. The director of the program may end it at any time, and invite the guests to try a few "biting" games. In several places in the hall, have doughnuts suspended on a string about the height of an average person's head; also apples the same way. The players have their hands tied behind them and try to bite the apple or doughnut as it swings merrily out of the way at each contact. Have also a raisin on a clean string, between two secure points, such as two husky freshmen. The players, one at each end of the string chew the string and see who gets to the raisin first. There may be several of these in operation. No prizes need be given, the fun being in the actions of the players.

GAME:—"SOCKING THE BAG"

Tie a large paper bag of wrapped candy like "Seafoam Kisses" or theatre chocolates, or peanuts, to a rope or strong cord, securely, to withstand shocks. The test is to break the bag in three shots with a ball or some similar object, at a reasonable distance from it, tossed and not thrown. If the bag is hit and not broken in three shots, it scores one point for a side; then the other side tries it. If the bag breaks, both sides scramble for the contents, and the fun is great as a clown falls madly over "Little Orphan Annie". If the bag remains stubbornly unbroken after the game has been going on for some time, it goes to the side making the most points, as a prize, and the sharing may be one-sided, if preferred.

WITCH GAME

Supply the guests with pointed paper witch hats, and pencils. On each witch hat five dots have been placed by the committee beforehand. The test of skill is to draw the best witch between the dots, that is using the dots to form the outline. The outline must be continuous from dot to dot but may wander off to one side to form the figure. The best drawing wins a prize of an artist's sketch or scrap book, the worst drawing a box of pencil erasers, the hint in using the erasers for poor work causing much fun. The witch hats are worn, if desired, through the evening, and retained as souvenirs.

GAME—"PUMPKIN INITIALS"

A large pumpkin is selected and the letters of the alphabet cut in it, or plainly painted on it in black. First a lady is invited to walk blindfolded and jab a hat pin into two letters on the pumpkins, these letters being a prophecy of what her future husband's name shall be—"C-S", perhaps, and

Charles Stevens, who is present, begins to feel jittery. A man is invited next and he finds his future wife's name in the same manner. The immediate reaction is to look around the company and see who possesses the fatal initials, and to read one's fate "on the spot".

GAME—"BLACK CAT RING"

Just before refreshments are served, have the guests seated in a ring close together, with lights low and spooky. Some one dressed as a witch announces that he will pass the various parts of a cat to the members of the ring, first the head to the first person in the ring. This person takes it and passes it to the next person, and so on. This is intended to be gruesome and about what any old witch would enjoy doing, for her boiling cauldron. The head is really a ball of soft yarn. The next is the eyes, or oysters; the next claws (bent hair pins); tail, (piece of old fur); insides (piece of dough); teeth (beads or beans); tongue, a pickle cut in half lengthwise; the hide is a large piece of fur. The shivery thrills in this stunt will probably be enough for the guests, and soon lights may be turned up, or on, and refreshments announced. Guests may remain in circle if desired, and be served on trays.

REFRESHMENTS: A Hallowe'en Revel calls for something tasty in the menu such as chicken sandwiches cut in circles, pumpkin pie and whipped cream and coffee. Sugared doughnuts or crullers and sweet cider may be served for a simple menu. Pop corn balls, delicious apples, and peanut brittle may be used also along with plain sandwiches and coffee. If cake is served, use yellow cakes with black and orange candies in the yellow icing, coffee, and large cream wafers made in yellow and orange colors, and mixed nuts.

"A Colonial Party"

A Colonial party should have all the glamour, the stately dances, the beautiful gowns of the ladies, the satin outfits the men wore in the early days, and above all the gay courageous spirit which really animated the colonists, and made them pause for pleasure amid dangers.

INVITATIONS: The invitations may be copies of samplers which sometimes may be found on store cards, or a sampler sketched in small size in ink on white cards. It need not be a perfect drawing, just a sketchy idea will do as well. With these words in the invitation, the acceptances should be many and spontaneous.

"A Colonial party will be given on November twentieth, at the home of Winnie Howe, at eight-thirty o'clock, Twenty Washington Avenue. You are cordially invited to come and sample ye olde tyme fun. Costumes appreciated."

DECORATIONS: For a Colonial party, in old New England style, the decorations may be quite elaborate, consisting of old silks, velvets, prints, whale oil lamps, candles in antique holders, old pictures, rugs, bed hangings, pewter dishes, rare old vases and pictures and antique settles and rockers. Some people do not like to loan these treasures, but others are willing to loan them if safety is guaranteed, and they do add much to the decorations. A few would answer the purpose in a home but larger things would be needed in a big hall. Select one type of decoration such as beautiful old pieces, and have nothing else. Or, choose the log cabin style of decoration, imitation snow, a wooden Indian, corn stalks, a wild turkey picture or two, rough benches, logs, outdoor fires in imitation, an old fire-arm, and a few real trees or shrubs. Colonial quilts are most attractive as decorations even at a party, for they may be draped in many beautiful ways; Plymouth Rock could be a grey cloth over a cushion or box; a ship model or picture of the Mayflower; cigar store wooden Indian partly concealed in shrubbery; Indian emblems and articles of dress; an iron kettle or two and imitation fire, snow banks of white cloth with evergreen branches over them, or a few real evergreen trees, and if desired, harvest products well arranged. With care, these suggestions may be adapted with clever results.

GAME:—"THE KING'S DECREES"

The first game is a novel one. Some one of the men should dress as a messenger from the king and rush in with great excitement and a sheaf of orders or decrees, to be carried out at once, on penalty of death or exile to England. To all the ladies give folded fans of stiff paper, with a different decree on each fan, or buy cheap fans and write the decrees on them in blood-red ink. To the men, present small snuff boxes with the decrees therein. A town crier should call out the names of the guests, and demand the carrying-out of the decree. Some of these decrees should be "wearing necktie crooked for the rest of the evening"; "Walk around the room like General Washington;" "act out John Alden and Priscilla"; "Capt. Smith and Pocohontas"; pose as "Squanto, the Indian friend of the colonists"; or as "Hannah Dustin with her hatchet with which she killed seven or more Indians while sleeping, on an island in the Merrimack River"; "wear a handkerchief on shoulder all the evening"; "tell the early history of the colonies in a few words"; "describe the Mayflower". There need be no prizes for this game as it is mostly to get the guests deeply into the spirit of early colonial days and ways.

GAME:—"COLONIAL WORD RACE"

Inviting the guests to be seated comfortably, pass long strips of paper in different colors, on the top of which have been glued heads cut from magazines, old-fashioned ones if possible. With pencils, the guests are to try a word race, writing upon their paper dolls all the words they can think of, ending in "ial". About fifteen minutes may be allowed for this word race, and some of the words are on this order:

Beastial	Perennial
Consequential	Social
Genial	Triennial

A first prize for the lady who writes the most words should be an early colonial picture, a Godey print, or Currier and Ives reproduction print. The first prize for the men should be a good pioneer book, a tale of the early days and the Indians.

DIVERSIONS: Throwing blue and buff discs into a basket that has been attached to the wall or set up high on a piece of furniture, for difficult aim. Choose sides and then have each side measure feet, is the next diversion. One foot is placed before the other, touching, and each side must see who can measure the farthest in "feet". This is highly amusing to all. Obtain a pewter plate or a large tin platter, and invite the guests to spin it, on a prescribed space, calling out the name of another guest before it stops spinning in order that he may be the one to try the stunt next. The object is to keep the plate or platter going constantly. Two plates, and sides, would make keen rivalry, and perhaps even more fun and exertion. A Colonial "T" party is a clever diversion, and a tongue-twister. Invite the guests to think up sentences, each word of which must begin with "T", as for instance:

"Thomas Tries To Turn Turtle."
"Theresa Tells Tales to Tabby."
"Tipsy Tabitha Thanked Thackeray."

After the sentences have been written on papers, shuffle them and give out for the guests to read aloud, as best they can.

GAME:—"A 'What-Not' Game"

The old what-nots of colonial days contained a grand litter of magazines, papers, trinkets, toys, and family accessories, in spite of mother's attempts to keep them neat and in order. For this game place on a table a box of toothpicks; a dish of marbles; a bunch of grapes; an umbrella; a paper weight; a bottle of camphor or vinegar, or both; a rubber ball; a roll of tape; a dish of baking soda. Other things may be used if one wishes to make the number of objects greater, or harder, to guess. The object is to tell on slips of paper how many toothpicks, how many marbles, how many grapes, how long the umbrella is, how heavy the paper weight, and so on. The articles or "what-nots" should be numbered, and the papers also. A first prize of a box of chocolate mints for the lady prize winner and a box of assorted nuts for a man winner should be given. There should be a time limit and no loitering at the table beyond reason. If desired, the players may be kept marching around the table to slow music, for too much time or closeness is not fair.

REFRESHMENTS: Old pewter dishes, tea in heavy mugs, buttered rolls, strawberry jam, pumpkin pie baked in individual ramekins, walnut halves, and sugared corn may constitute one menu. In a hall, soft drinks, gingerbread doll cookies, sandwiches of many kinds, cream cheese made into balls and rolled in crushed cinnamon candies, coffee, and ices in log cabin molds on spun glass. Old-fashioned china dishes of any kind are lovely to use, or paper sets of fancy design, if more convenient, and in buff and blue colors. Napkins may have small turkeys on them. Guests may be partnered for refreshments by having a minuet and when the music stops suddenly, chose present partner. Souvenirs of blue and buff ribbon bows for boutonnieres, would be a delightful gesture.

"A Spring Round-Up Party"

When the spring or Easter vacation is over, it is a good time to round up the class members for a general conference and social affair that will revive class spirit. Parties have been prevalent during the spring recess for individuals, but for the class as a whole, there should be a get-together a short time after studies have been resumed.

INVITATIONS: For this spring round-up, have "riders" sent out to deliver the invitations, if possible, in person. Select cream-colored cards and in one corner, paint a ten-gallon hat in water colors, in tan or grey. For the style of wording, the following may be used:

"You are urgently invited to the Bar-None Ranch of Fred Wood, Talman County Range, two hours after sunset, on April twentieth, Six Sumner Avenue. R.S. V.P. or 'Ride South Via Pell Mell!' Costumes."

DECORATIONS: A spring round-up party should carry out western ideas of plains, prairies, cowboys, ranch girls, ponies and corrals, and so forth. In one corner of the room set up a small tree from the woods, with or without leaves, and on it hang a sign "Bar-None Ranch". Have two good men singers who can also strike a few chords on a guitar or banjo, reclining under the tree, dressed in cowboy regalia and their big hats hung up on the tree, while they sing some of the familiar radio cowboy songs such as "Empty Saddles in the Old Corral", "Git Along Little Dogie", "Old Faithful", "Wagon Wheels", "Home on the Range", or "The Last Round-Up" in soft low singing tones. Around the rooms arrange men's large colored handkerchiefs, in fancy designs like fans, bows, table covers, cushion covers, and so forth. Have pictures of buffalo and wild game, here and there, and a few old-time pictures of the inns and stopping-places of wild-west days; Buffalo Bill in person in his picturesque costume. If there is a class artist who will donate his talent, have him make western sketches, just rough drawings which he may copy from authentic histories of the west, and place these around the rooms or hall for the enjoyment of the guests. Early spring does not produce many flowers for decorative purposes, but there are a few small varieties, and poppies or hardy blue phlox which may be sometimes obtained in April. The artificial spring flowers are quite satisfactory and may be used in a rather sparing way for this kind of party perhaps for the refreshment table decoration. The idea of a western setting, like the wide bare plains or far-flung grassy ranges, will be more appropriate and interesting to guests.

GAME:—"THE COVERED WAGON"

Give to each guest a placard on which is printed the name of some part of a covered wagon of pioneer days, such as an axle, wheel, spring, body, seat, hub, spokes, nuts, bolts, pins, and so forth and to one person the name "covered wagon". Have a good story-teller read in an abbreviated form, the story of "The Covered Wagon", and as various parts of a covered wagon are read, the persons representing the parts must stand up quickly or pay a forfeit. If the story is well and speedily read, the players are almost sure to forget to rise. Forfeits should be paid at once and should be short and quickly performed like "untying a shoe lace", going to a certain person and saying, "Howdy, old pal", or patting a person on the head three times, or reciting a poem, or bowing six times. Any little funny forfeits will do, and a score-keeper keeps track of the forfeits paid by each player. The winner is the player with the least or no forfeits, and receives a copy of "The Covered Wagon" in book form or a western story by some well-known author.

GAME:—"A RANCH RACE"

Divide the guests into two groups or select two men to be leaders of groups. The leaders choose players for their sides. Then the leaders go out of the room. Each side chooses a certain letter. That is, one side, representing Bar-X Ranch, chooses "B" and the other group, Bar-O Ranch, chooses "C". The leaders return and each tries to guess what the letter of his side is, first, by calling out words, as "spring", "tourist", and so forth. The leader who gets to the right letter first, wins for his side. Questions by the leaders are permitted to help them guess. This stunt may be repeated with new leaders each time. If preferred, each side may decide on some ranch object for guessing such as cabin, bunk, coral, prairie, rope, rodeo, and so on, and ask the leaders to guess it. Each leader takes turn in guessing.

GAME:—"THE RANCH RODEO"

One person is selected as a leader. Each player is given the name of some part of a rodeo, such as rope, steer, stirrup, horse, saddle, spur, hat, coat, boots, and if desired, any other names as mane, hoofs, horns. The leader tells his story of a rodeo and as he calls out various things, the players bearing those names must run and stand behind the leader with one hand on the shoulder of the person in front of him. The leader calls fast "my hat", "my lariat", the "steer is rarin' to go", and when all players are out of their chairs, the leader calls out, very suddenly, "rodeo" and all scramble back for a chair. One chair has, however, been removed so that someone gets left at the "rodeo" and has to become the leader. This continues for awhile until the players are ready for a more quiet game.

GAME:—"WHAT CAN YOU SHOOT WITH?"

Give out papers and pencils and ask each player to write down the names of all the things one can shoot with, such as, rifle, revolver, gun, arrow and bow, pop-gun, sling-shot, cannon, etc. Give a time allowance of about ten minutes for this game, and the player who thinks of the most things, should be awarded a fine school notebook. The second highest number, possibly a girl, should receive a fine school tablet. If it is desired to have a little fun with the prizes, award a toy water pistol and a bean blower. Prizes for this short stunt should not be elaborate.

DIVERSIONS: Lay several pieces of rope in loops along the floor, and ask a blindfolded person to walk ten or twelve feet without stepping in a noose or trap. He will go through many strange antics and motions and facial expressions. Before he reaches his goal, and when he has the handkerchief removed from his eyes, he is quietly told all the nooses were removed before he started, so his contortions were in vain, but that the company thoroughly enjoyed his performance just the same! Half the fun of this stunt is to have the guests make all sorts of encouraging remarks to the "victim", and his sincere appreciation of same and renewed efforts to be "careful", are hilarious fun for the onlookers. Two people might do this stunt at the same time.

A mock trial at this round-up party might be much enjoyed and prove very funny. If given in a hall, preparations for it should be more detailed but for a home, some one who has the gift of impersonation should be the judge and conduct the trial, in a simple way, such as, "Mary Lane is up before the court for running a music hall too near the Bar-None Ranch boundary lines." Witnesses are called, a jury impanelled, prosecution and defense pleas are made, and the jury brings in a verdict. Poor Mary is acquitted but fined ten cents and costs for disturbing the peace of Bar-None Ranch boys. All in the spirit of fun. Another diversion may be an indoor target and soft-tipped arrows that will test the skill of the guests.

GAME:—"HIDDEN OBJECT"

While the guests are comfortably seated, one person goes into another room out of hearing. The players in this game decide on some object near at hand which is at the same time, hidden from view, such as the handkerchief in a player's coat pocket, the compact in a girl's purse, a dime in a person's hand, a magazine under a rug. The person who is to guess comes in and by adroit questioning tries to guess what the hidden object may be. The game is more difficult when the object is hidden but if more enjoyable, an object may be chosen which is in view all the time. Either way the game is kept snappy by clever questioning and cautious answers till the object is finally guessed correctly.

REFRESHMENTS: For a spring round-up party it is well to have some of the new spring products that may be in the market, if they are not too expensive. The first strawberries used in a crushed form with sugar, on ice cream, are always hailed with delight. Use green glass serving plates, green sherbet glasses, vanilla ice cream with fresh crushed strawberry; serve with cakes topped with white icing and candied cherries, on green glass cake dishes; white cream peppermint candy and wintergreen in deep pink, or cinnamon-red cream wafers in green glass candy dishes; cashew nuts in a green glass bowl with fancy spoon, and coffee. The napkins may be bright green paper napkins folded into a roll, tied with red and white ribbon and placed in a large green glass dish which may serve as a centerpiece. Refreshments may be served at a large round dining table and a round-table conference be conducted at the same time, sort of a round-up of spring recess doings, opinions, and plans for future days as a class. In this case the serving should be done by persons engaged for the purpose so that all the class members may be able to be together and answer "present" at the Round-Up roll call. This round-up should be on the order of a regular class meeting, with the president in the chair and necessary old business disposed of and new business considered, and other routine matters. If it is to be the last regular class meeting of the year, close the affair by all singing "The Last Round-Up", a stirring song for a lively party and an all-round good time.

"A Flower Festival"

A flower festival may be carried out at any time of the year, but in June it might be most appropriate because graduation means farewell and nothing expresses words of farewell or "auf wiedersehen" so well as the language of flowers. Class members are fatigued by the studies of the long school year, the warm weather of June days, and the stimulus of a lovely flower party would be both beneficial and delightful.

INVITATIONS: The invitations should be on cream-colored cards with the class flower in water color in the corner of the card. If the class does not possess a flower emblem, use the red rambler rose for the party flower and paint it in the form of a spray across the card. The invitation wording may take the form of four lines of some well-known poem on June, or it may be worded as follows:

"Our class will conduct a flower festival at the home
of Mildred Watson on Friday evening at eight o'clock,
June eighteenth, at Number Five Providence Avenue.
Please try to be present at our flower festival—WE
WANT YOU!"

DECORATIONS: One's fancy may run free in arranging decorations for a flower festival but it is best to choose a theme and abide by it. If the red rambler rose is to be the theme, it should work out beautifully. Use plain jardinieres, vases, bowls and tall slender vases for sprays of this showy flower, not too many but wisely placed to show to the best advantage against plain backgrounds of dark color. Greens may be used profusely when this party is to be given in a hall, and in a home, ferns, tall baskets of laurel leaves and rhododendron are very effective in corners or archways. If not possible to get enough rambler rose for a decorative scheme buy artificial sprays of red flowers or red roses, but keep the color scheme red and green. It is very rich and lovely for a June party. Nothing else is needed in the way of decoration but the flowers and the greens.

GAME:—"NAMING THE FLOWERS"

For this game, purchase as many green paper drinking cups as possible. Perhaps thirty or forty would do. Then purchase artificial flowers of thirty or forty varieties in the ten-cent store. Buy the familiar ones with a few hard ones to guess for "stickers". Put one flower, plant, or spray in each cup after cutting a round of cardboard to fit into each cup with a hole in it to hold the flower fairly firm and upright. Arrange these on a large table or on several small tables for a guessing game. The guests are given red and green-colored papers and pencils and are asked to name the flowers on exhibition in fifteen minutes time. The first prize for a girl should be a small growing plant and for a man a small package of grass seed or a wall flower holder for his own room at home. The consolation prize may be a packet of seeds. The game is not too difficult for a starter, is attractive, and not so easy to do as one might think.

GAME:—"FLOWER LANGUAGE"

When all the guests are seated, distribute to them artificial flowers two only of each kind, and attached to these flowers have a strip of strong green paper or cardboard which provides something to write upon, and a pencil. A leader reads off the questions and the players are given about two or three minutes to guess the flower and write it down.

1. What does Johnny do when he sits on a tack?
                              Johnny-jump-up.
2. An early riser and an implement to make a horse go?
                              Larkspur.
3. An early bird and and a hair implement? ....Cockscomb.
4. A flower of the low lands? ....Valley lily.

5. What a cat talks with? ....Cat Tail.
6. Something good on bread and to make cake?
                                                    Buttercup.
7. What a masked man says, and something cracked?
                                                    Forget-me-*nut*.
8. An alphabet letter with a nice odor? ....Sweet pea.
9. A flashily-dressed man and a jungle animal? Dandelion.
10. What mother uses on Willie? ....Lady's Slipper.
11. A man with a good disposition? ....Sweet William.
12. Why do dukes prefer rich wives? ....Marigold.
13. A tramp bird? ....Ragged Robin.
14. A yellow cane? ....Golden Rod.
15. A lady who won't flirt? ....Primrose.

There are many flowers with a language of their own, and the above may be extended, shortened, or changed, as preferred. The prizes should be artistic, a small colored picture of flowers, or a tinted garden picture for the lady winner and a flower-decorated necktie holder for a man, with consolation prize of a bunch of wild flowers, real or artificial.

DIVERSIONS: Since the guests already have two flowers of a kind, invite them to partner off by matching flowers, the men having been given one set of flowers for the above game, and the girls the other set. Have two strings stretched tightly across the room, and on each string a light-weight flower. The flower may be caught on very lightly so that it will blow easily. Have one couple at each string, the object being to blow the flower along the string to the goal.

Names of flowers, in letters that may be read easily, but have the letters mixed up. Place these letters on the backs of guests with pins, the letters may be printed, if desired, on papers. The idea is to guess what flower the letters represent. The one who wears the letter may ask questions in order to discover what his own flower name may be.

Form a circle or ring. A leader walks around and drops an artificial flower and says the name of a flower three times before the one to whom the flower is dropped can say it once. This stunt calls for alertness and a quick tongue. Failure to say the name of the flower once, in time, makes the player "it".

GAME:—"FLOWER-FACES"

Cut large flowers from florists' catalogues and faces of well-known people from magazines. Paste the faces in the centers of the flowers and pass these to the guests to name correctly, on slips of paper which have been properly numbered. The face of Will Rogers in a poppy; of the president in a rose; of Wallace Berry in a sunflower, and Edna Ferber in a dahlia will create lots of fun. A prize of a small dish in the shape of a flower for a girl winner, and a cigar tray in the shape of a flower for a man, would be appropriate for this guessing game. If partners have been retained, this game becomes quite enjoyable, getting the answers together.

REFRESHMENTS: These should be very attractive if served at small tables, each table representing a flower, a sort of festival of gay blooms such as golden glow, rose, lily, pansy, iris, phlox, nasturtiums and others. Crepe paper lunch sets may be used, or sets of linen or plain colors to carry out the color chosen for each table. Yellow dishes on the golden glow tables, lavender on the pansy, blue on the phlox, white on the lily tables would indeed be a riot of color. If it seems more convenient, the original color scheme may be maintained even to the refreshments, green lunch sets and red-decorated glass serving dishes of which there are many patterns in the stores. The menu for a flower festival in June may be simple and served in crepe-paper covered strawberry baskets if preferred such as several sandwiches, a large slice of cake, and fancy cookies all wrapped in cellophane or in the wax paper that comes decorated in lovely colors and designs. Candy and nuts and one piece of fruit may be in the baskets. These baskets may be passed informally, and will be a pleasant surprise. If the small tables are more convenient, serve ices in molded flower forms on spun glass. They are delicious and beautiful. Two kinds of cake and coffee with the ices is a very appropriate and sufficient menu for this flower party. Centerpieces for each small table may be candy flowers in cellophane wrappers, two of a kind so that they may be presented to the two ladies at each table as favors. Class songs are a happy ending to this party.

"A Box Party"

A Box Party may be given at any time of the year and to make it distinctive may be called a Thanksgiving, Christmas, New Year or Easter Box Party, with decorations and features characteristic of those holiday seasons as added attractions. It may also take the form of a Poverty, Charity, or Birthday Box Party, if desired to use it as a means of obtaining money for community interests or for replenishing the class treasury.

INVITATIONS: For a general Box Party the invitations should be a square of paper with four sides and flaps which when folded properly or glued will form a small box. On the flat paper box write the following words:

"Come to my Box Party
And bring some cents.
Home of Marion Allston, Five Adams Avenue, Friday
Evening, the tenth, at Half-Past Eight O'Clock.
Come early, stay late!
Your pennies we'll take
At the Box-Office gate."

DECORATIONS: For a general Box Party, the decorations should be strong boxes for chairs, covered with rugs, cushions, or cloth. Box hedge plants may be used in boxes filled with dirt, and wrapped around with colored paper, and tied with gay ribbons. Egg boxes may be covered with colored paper and have artificial or real flowers or plants in each small section. If boxes are to be covered with paper, select a color scheme for the purpose—red, white, and blue, or the class colors, or black and white, and adhere to this color scheme in all details. There are beautiful gold and silver papers, Christmas papers, and fancy wax papers with lovely designs on them. Large boxes may be used as tables, especially when the Box Party is to be given in a hall. In a home, the decorations should be kept clever, simple and attractive, using only enough boxes to emphasize your idea.

GAME—"BOXED PRODUCTS"

Give to the guests long strips of paper and pencils, and invite them to write their names in large letters on the tops, then to list as many products as they can think of in a given time, such as candy, matches, tea, cereal, and so forth. The longest list wins a box of Nabisco wafers, the next a box of matches, and the shortest a playful "box" on the ears.

GAME—"ADJECTIVES BY THE BOX"

While guests are still seated, ask the players to tear off their names from the tops of the lists, or a helper may do this. Pass a box and ask the men to put their names in it; a box for the girls' names, also. The leader and her helper then draw a man's name and a girl's, and from the list of adjectives prepared beforehand, couple number one is described as "gentle", "snippy," "aristocratic"—as their luck may be. The leader and her helper should read in a clear voice, jolly and snappy, to give the proper "swing" to the game. No offensive adjectives are permitted, of course.

GAME—"SUIT BOX RACE"

Procure several pasteboard suit boxes. In half of them place a maid's uniform, cap and apron with long strings. In the other half, place a chef's uniform, tall white hat (paper or stiff cloth) and a big white apron not too hard to get into. Invite the guests to form into two groups as they choose. Start two couples in the race, if possible; if not, one couple, from a home goal line, and give to the man a box with a maid's uniform, and to the girl, a box with a chef's uniform. The instructions are to race to goal number two, open the boxes, don the uniforms correctly and return to the home goal. The first couple back, correctly uniformed, scores five points for their group. If only one couple at a time may race, individual winner scores five points for his group, if good; the not-so-good racer gets only three points for his particular group. Continue until all contestants have entered the race. This provides plenty of action, and the uniforms may be exchanged, and another heat run off. While the guests are taking time out to regain their breath, award one carmel for each point attained by each group. There will be without doubt caramels enough for all, win or lose.

GAME—"MAGIC FORTUNE BOXES"

The committee should make an extra supply of small paper boxes when the invitations are being prepared. On each side of the extra set, print a large letter such as "A, P, P, L, E", and on the lid of the box write "a fruit". Inside the glued or pasted boxes, place a clever fortune, suitable for either man or girl, such as "you have the faculty of making money, also of losing it. Beware the stock market"! "You make friends easily. Beware of a friend with dark eyes and light hair." Pass the small boxes to guests and suggest that they form the large letters on the sides into a word suggested on the lid or top, and only after they have gotten the word out correctly, may they open their boxes and read their fortunes.

DIVERSIONS: If it seems advisable to ask the guests to move about, try a Blind Man's Boxing contest. Provide a large covered box, a pair of boxing gloves, and two blindfolded men, and let them go to it around the big box. The first blow counts one, five blows is "out". The guests will be "close seconds" in the diversion. Referee fairly. If desired to obtain money for the class treasury or for charity, pass small mite or coin boxes for the guests to put in their cents which they brought to the party. If it is a Birthday Box Party, pennies according to age may be brought and donated. For a Christmas Box Party the boxes of pennies may be given to a Rotary, Kiwanis, or Quota Club for distribution to poor children in the form of toys.

Another diversion may be trying to balance a matchbox on nose or little finger and pass it to next player. A small paper box may be used in the same way. Still another diversion may be a large box with slot in it to hold the names of the most popular man and girl present, each guest entitled to cast one vote for each.

GAME—"SHOE BOX RACE"

Provide several shoe boxes, a race track, a referee, and ask for volunteers to "hoof it" down the track, one foot or "hoof" in each shoe box. In a hall, this would be a delightful exhibition; in a home it would probably be a struggle to make progress, and just as funny—for the "fans". A prize of a shoe box full of candied popcorn would be appropriate and it might also be passed around and help out on the refreshments. A box of "ironized yeast" tablets might "pep" up the loser.

GAME—"VANITY BOX RACE"

Place six or eight boxes of different sizes on the floor and call for volunteers to "hop to it" and limber up by hopping on one foot over and around each box from one to eight, but not touching a box. If the guests feel too much "heated up" after two races, allow a cooling off spell, and provide a guessing game.

GAME—"HOW MANY BOXES?"

The leader should ask the first player to name one word beginning with "box", such as "boxer", and so on around the circle, there being many such names. Box office, boxberry, box coat, Boxer, a Chinese Society, boxing, boxwood, and at least ten uses of the word "box" alone which comes from the Latin word "buxus". During this quieting game, the committee should bring in the refreshments in boxes, two of each color or kind, and provide strips of paper, two of a color, which should be passed to each guest in deep boxes, the guests partnering by the simple method of taking out a colored strip of paper, the men from one box, the girls from another box.

REFRESHMENTS: The boxes may be made quite delightful, both as a novelty and as to good refreshments. They should be the square pasteboard boxes that are used in bakeries for cakes and pies, and should have the color on them either in large circles pasted on, or tied up with colored ribbon, two of a color. Inside each box place a gay paper napkin, a paper cup of potato salad and a wooden spoon—these wooden spoons may be bought in cellophane bags of twenty for five cents—a small roll buttered and containing chopped meat or a meat paste, one sweet pickle, a cocoanut cup cake, a small cellophane bag of candy, and one of nuts, and a plain bread and butter sandwich. Coffee may be served, or iced drinks which are somewhat more convenient to hold with a refreshment box, a tall glass with a straw or long spoon. The box party will be complete if some one starts a favorite class song, or an impromptu serenade to the committee.

"A Mystery Party"

Everyone likes a mystery! Strange doings, strange noises! How many thrills are experienced when the ghost of Mystery walks! And so there is no party more enjoyable than a mystery party, and it is well worth the efforts of the committee to work up all the novelties possible, conjure up a few ghosts, real or impersonated, invent a few "scrapings" and "fillings" and "groans", and see how admirably the guests will shiver and shake with real or. pretended fear.

INVITATIONS: The invitations should be of a clever design for this party, a good idea being to have the outside envelope marked with lines, and so forth, to represent a box. Then inside, have another smaller envelope like a box, and so on, down to a tiny envelope with the words inside on a folded strip of paper:

"Come to my Mystery Party on October X at X plus 5 Winton Avenue, at X minus 3 o'clock. To meet "Mr. A." informally.
Margaret Weiss   R.S.V.P.

DECORATIONS: For a mystery party, there should be screens around the rooms, and behind the screens have small tables with various articles upon them that are mysterious-looking, that emit sounds, or are queer to the touch. Many such objects may be obtained in a store easily, or they may be procured at home, such as a cake with a chimney, windows, and so forth, in it, a clock ticking in a closed tin box; a piece of soap cut in some odd shape as an animal. These things may be seen and tested in a very dim light. Another screen may conceal "Mr. A." which may be anything beginning with "A" but might be a baby alligator from one of the southern alligator farms. These may be obtained for one dollar and thirty-five cents, sent well packed and guaranteed to live or be replaced. A sheet may be hung up and different kinds of lights placed behind it as kerosene lamp, candy, flashlight, electric bulb and so forth. Decorations of a less novel nature may be large baskets of greens from the woods, or autumn leaves on large branches.

PARTNERS: The guests should be invited to find partners by choosing a mystery bag which will contain the future of each one, that is, the profession or trade of the man who will be the lady's choice at some future day. These bags should be hung from a line strung along the wall and each lady selects the bag she wishes. Upon opening the bag, she finds a measuring tape for a civil engineer; a small hammer for a carpenter; a pen for a writer; a book for a librarian; nuts and bolts for· a mechanic, and other objects indicative of a trade or profession. The men choose envelopes containing the same trades, and thus find their partners easily.

GAME—"THE MYSTERY MEMORY TEST"

This game is one to test the speed, accuracy and memory of the guests. Upon a large table arrange many objects, at least twenty-five or thirty, and these may be varied, large or small, and of different shape and color, such as a piece of coal, ruler, eraser, match, pipe, tapioca, cotter pin, nails, beads, brush and other objects to make the game more difficult. Two or three couples at a time may look at the objects which are covered at first, then the cover is removed for a minute, and replaced. This gives the players the chance to memorize the names of the objects and write them down correctly. The players should stand the same distance from the table. If the table is large enough, all the guests may view the objects at the same time. About ten minutes should be allowed for writing the names, or as long as the hostess wishes, but if too much time is given the game is rather too easy. A first prize given is a mystery package, containing a gift for a man and a girl winner. A consolation prize of a paper bag of pop corn or salted peanuts may be awarded.

GAME—"MYSTERY STUNTS"

Each couple is requested to do some sort of a stunt for the other guests to guess. For instance, a couple may decide to do a "cake walk", another couple may be good dancers and impersonate Fred Astaire and Ginger Rogers; another couple may choose to imitate Amos and Andy on the radio; another may imitate driving a Ford car, with plenty of imitation rattles, whoas, and so forth, meaning an oldtime car, of course, not the new luxurious type. Another couple may choose to act out an evening in the movies, or boxing, or pulling candy, and so forth, almost any clever stunt will do, but it should be well chosen and not too easy to guess. No prizes are needed for there will be plenty of fun watching the players perform.

GAME—"WHOOPEE GAME"

Give to each player a card about five inches square with twenty-five inch squares marked upon it. In each square put any number up to fifty and arrange the numbers so that each square has a different number. Each card must also be different from any of the others as to numbers upon it and arrangement of them. A leader shakes a number from a box of pasteboard numbers, and calls out—"thirteen"! Each player is given peas and places one on number thirteen square on his card. The box is again shaken and "twenty-two" is called out. The first person to get a full line of peas, either across, down, or diagonally, calls out "Whoopee!" and wins the round. The game goes on, and the person winning the most rounds at the end of a specified time, receives a prize of a box of peanut brittle. A consolation prize may be a peanut bar.

DIVERSIONS: If "Mr. A." has been kept a secret up to this time, the guests should be asked to suggest any name that begins with "A", and the nearest correct name should be first introduced to "Mr. A." behind the scenes (or screen). The guests will be properly loud and enthusiastic over the meeting, and then without revealing the mystery, the other guests are introduced in groups.

A laugh-provoking diversion is to scatter about twenty or thirty peas on an old rug and ask the guests to spear them with hatpins or other sharp instruments. This is quite hard to do, and if desired to make it easier, peanuts in the shell or cranberries may be used. Not too much time can be allowed for spearing.

The first player in a circle takes a paper with a word on it in large letters as "America". Then he holds the paper upside down in his left hand and says, "he can read little who can't read this", and passes it to the next player to do as he did. The next person will read the letters correctly, and probably hold the paper upside down as he repeats the word, but fails to hold the paper in his left hand at the same time.

GAME—"MYSTERY TRADES OR PROFESSIONS"

This should be a lively game and requires clever action, either by couples, by groups, or by sides, as may be decided by the hostess. The idea is to act out trades in pantomime, singing, conversation, tableau, recitation or any other form that may be decided upon by players. There is a mysterious trade hidden in the actions of the players and the fun is in selecting a good trade to present, but a hard one to guess. Of course, the usual easy trades of laundress, dressmaker, shoemaker, writer may be acted out, but it would be more in the spirit of this mystery party to act out mysterious trades, such as magician, a radio announcer, a teacher of an uncommon subject, a mechanic, a hairdresser or cosmetician, a motorman, a bricklayer, a banker, a postman, an author, a poet and so on. These may sound easy to guess but they should be difficult if they are presented in some unexpected way. Prizes are not needed for this game but it might add to the fun to have the players who present the best line of trades or professions served by the losing side when refreshments are in order.

REFRESHMENTS: For a mystery party the refreshments should consist of coffee and cakes containing mysterious objects baked in them, as a tiny china doll, a ring, a fancy brooch, a twenty-five cent piece, a pearl button, or any object that will bear a careful cleaning before baking in the cakes, and that is large enough to be found readily. Guests should be advised that objects are hidden in the cakes, since part of the fun is anticipation. Sandwiches of sliced meats may be used, and one or two sandwiches may be announced as mystery sandwiches, containing a mysterious filling (a thin piece of cloth carefully placed between bread slices). Those who get the mystery sandwiches should be awarded "consolation" prizes of small cellophane bags of olives, as "fillers", and of course, genuine sandwiches that they can eat. The idea of a mystery party is one of unexpected things happening, and the guests should be "kept guessing" as well as entirely happy, through all the games and stunts.

"An Easter Party"

The goddess of spring, Eostre, celebrates her festival in April, on the first Sunday after the full moon of March twenty-first or later, and to be right in the spirit of the beautiful Easter time, a party should take place just before the general observance of Easter. Easter is a season of happiness and a party planned with due regard for its reverent aspect will in no way be solemn, but should prove of real joy and gladness, with friendly contacts which make Easter really worth while.

INVITATIONS: The invitations for the party should be attractive Easter cards such as may be purchased quite easily, with envelopes to match. On the cards write or print in rather large letters the following words:

"You are cordially invited to an Easter party to be given at the home of Evelyn Watson, Number Ten Harrison Avenue, on Friday evening, March twenty-fifth at eight-thirty o'clock. Please bring an Easter "bunny" card.   R.S.V.P."

Cut the invitations into several odd shapes, perhaps eight in all, to serve as an Easter puzzle to those invited, but a puzzle very quickly "pieced together" and followed with pleasure. If the committee prefers, paper bunnies may be used on which to write the invitations. These may be easily cut out of all colors of paper, with one or two bunnies as patterns to lay on several thicknesses of paper. The wording to be the same.

DECORATIONS: For decorations, small potted plants of cineraria, daffodils, tulips, or mixed spring flowers from a florist should constitute a feature, and after the party is over, sent to any class members who are ill as a gift. If possible, the color scheme should be confined to pink and yellow. Streamers of pink and yellow bunting or crepe paper may be twisted and hung from the tops of window casings to the floor like soft draperies and tied back with large bows. Pink and yellow paper shades for lamps may be used in place of the regular shades or over them. The potted plants should be arranged in a mass on a table like a flower garden, with a border of greens from the woods around them. Other decorations may be one or two well-filled Easter baskets, large chocolate bunnies and small ones, in various places and a paper hen cut from a magazine, eyeing a small nest of brilliantly-colored eggs— in blank surprise! Pink and yellow candles with huge bows of gauze ribbon add a festive touch, and if artificial flowers are to be used, large centerpieces of pink and yellow flowers combined, give a showy effect for the gay Easter time and are inexpensive.

GAME—"BIBLE TREES AND PLANTS"

The first contest consists of a large table with about twenty-five products representing the trees and plants named in the Bible. These products may be displayed in small paper dishes, and should be numbered to correspond with the following list, and also have a description typed or written on small cards and placed with each product. The number may be on the same card with the description, if desired. A first prize for the nearest correct list of names may be a bottle of olives, one of the Bible products, which has been dressed up in yellow crepe paper and tied with a large pink ribbon bow, to which is attached a card saying "olives, first prize". A second prize— for it is quite difficult to recall the trees and plants mentioned in the Bible—should be a small bottle of walnut meats, dressed up exactly like the first prize and labelled. A consolation prize of an apple, a Bible fruit, should be given. This game requires some time but the guests enjoy looking over the products as well as trying to guess the names.

1. Native trees of Palestine, blossoms before the leaves are out. Jeremiah. Answer—Almond tree.
2. In Matthew. Answer—Anise.
3. Shade tree, attractive, delicious fruit. Mentioned in Songs of Solomon. Answer—Apple.
4. Tree from which idols were made. Isaiah. Answer—Ash.
5. Common in Palestine as food for men and beasts. Used as a mark of poverty and worthlessness. Ruth and Judges. Answer—Barley.
6. A luguminous plant of Palestine, used for food and in flour. Samuel. Ezekiel. Answer—Bean.
7. Forest tree from which combs, spoons, etc., were made. Grew on Mt. Lebanon. Isaiah. Answer—Box.
8. Aromatic reed from which fragrant essence was extracted. Jeremiah. Songs of Solomon. Answer—Sweet Cane.
9. Tree something like laurel from which perfume was made. It was also an ingredient of the Holy Oil. Exodus. Proverbs. Answer—Cinnamon.
10. Most common of the orange tribe in Palestine. Occasionally used in synagogue worship as representative of God's gift of fruits. Leviticus. Answer—Citron.
11. Grain. Numbers. Judges. Answer—Corn.
12. Aromatic plant growing wild in Palestine. Used in medicine. Matthew. Answer—Dill.
13. Choice and goodly tree used for building purposes. Isaiah. Answer—Fir.
14. General term for water weeds. Exodus. Jonah. Answer—Flag.
15. Food for the extreme poor. Eighteen species found in Palestine. Job. Answer—Mallow.
16. Commonly eaten by Jews with meat. One of the bitter herbs of the Paschal Feast. Several species in Palestine. Luke. Answer—Mint.
17. Annual herb with very small seeds. Grew in Palestine. Matthew. Answer—Mustard.
18. One of the earliest trees named. One of the special blessings of the promised land. Very abundant in

Palestine. Genesis. Deut. Answer—Olive.

19. Preservative against thirst. Vegetable of Egypt. Numbers. Answer—Onion.

20. Scented garden flower, species of crocus which grew in Palestine. A yellow powder. Was used for seasoning in the east. Songs of Solomon. Answer—Saffron.

21. Palestine noted for the quality, quantity, and productiveness of its growth. It was the emblem of the nation. Genesis. Deut. Answer—Vine.

22. Tree native to Persia. Cultivated also in Palestine. Songs of Solomon. Answer—Walnut tree.

23. Chief grain in Jacob's time. Three varieties in Palestine. The harvesting of this grain marked a division of the year. Genesis. Answer—Wheat.

After the guests have spent as much time as the hostess thinks best on the above guessing game, they may be comfortably seated and try their powers of dexterity on the following game.

GAME—"THE MAGIC EGGS"

The leader explains that one of the eggs must be gently handled for fear of disaster, and then passes an egg to the first player on each side or team, stating that players must pass the eggs safely to the next players and count up to ten before the leader blows a tin horn as a signal. The players should not be seated too close to each other so that the leader can watch the passing of the eggs from one to another—and no false moves allowed! The object is to see which side gets the egg safely to the last player, in the shortest time and with the fewest points. A time keeper is on hand and a score keeper for each side. Failure to get the egg passed and count ten, both before the horn is blown, counts five points against that side. The result is generally a high nervous tension over the safety of the eggs, and the fun is great. At the end of the game, of course, the leader announces that *both* eggs are hard boiled and all the worry has been useless. No prizes are necessary, the actions of the players being highly satisfactory and delightful.

GAME—"EASTER EGG HUNT"

The leader announces the egg hunt with the following "short story". "The Easter egg as a gift is a custom which originated before Christianity. The egg was regarded as a symbol of new life, appropriate for Easter time and the birth of spring, and came to be colored mostly to give added pleasure to young children." All the eggs have been boiled hard, colored, and hidden securely about the rooms by the committee. On each egg has been placed two initials—of each guest who has been invited. Only one egg may be found by each player, who at once takes a seat until all the eggs have been found by the guests. The leader then provides pencils and papers and asks each player to answer her questions in two words beginning with initials on the egg found by player.

1. What does your friend look like? Like Heck.
2. What is his or her pet hobby? Licking Honey.
3. What is his or her greatest ambition? Lifting Horses.

These three examples illustrate the questionnaire and form of answers, L. H. being the two initials used for an example. The leader collects papers, shuffles them, and passes them out again, then calls out "L. H. Lydia Holmes." The player having L. H. reads aloud the idiosyncrasies of Lydia Holmes, much to the amusement of Miss Holmes and the other guests.

DIVERSIONS: A jar on a table filled with candy Easter eggs, the number to be guessed by players, and a prize of a box of them to be given to the one who guesses nearest the correct number. Two goals of books piled upon the floor. The game is to fan an egg into the goals. The egg should be whole with contents carefully removed, to make it light. Newspapers may be used for fans. An egg race may be staged, blown eggs to be carried on small spoons from one goal to another, safely and with speed. Shortest time wins the race. Spatulas may be used instead of spoons.

Conveying an egg in the same way from the floor to a table and putting in a bowl causes some little excitement.

PARTNERS: Paper rabbit ears may be provided, two of a color, and the guests asked to choose, the men from one set, the girls from another. When partnered, the couples are given a large puzzle, one for each couple, to put together in the shape of an Easter bunny. The first couple to succeed is escorted to the dining room, and gets first choice of the refreshments. Needless to say there will be speed and flurry in this method of being accessible to the refreshments. Puzzles should not be too complicated, of course. Guests are requested to wear the paper rabbit ears into the dining room.

REFRESHMENTS: In the center of the dining room table, a centerpiece is arranged with a large box containing the "bunny" cards which guests were requested in the invitations to bring. The box is decorated with Easter flowers and crepe paper and bears a sign "To be given to the children of the Mercy Hospital". The menu consists of very small dainty chicken sandwiches; the next course, Easter lilies in molded ices on spun glass, and these are most attractive and delicious; gold and silver cake; mixed Kashew and almond nuts, and coffee. A more simple menu may be a generous supply of biscuit in which a small sausage has been baked, brought in and served very hot after the guests are seated. These are substantial and require only coffee and small iced cup cakes to accompany them. Yellow baskets such as may be had in any variety store for a small sum should be at each place, on pink lace paper doilies, filled with candy and nuts. The puzzle players who speeded up for refreshments really get only the little baskets for their pains, until the rest are served. After the guests have enjoyed the refreshments for awhile, the hostess may read a short sketch about Easter Island, a spot that probably few people realized ever existed.

EASTER ISLAND

Easter Island is in the South Pacific Ocean. The inhabitants are Malayo-Polynesians, not many more than a hundred or two in all. The highest point on the island is 1200 feet. The soil is fertile but cultivation is rare. The island belongs to Chile and is used for grazing purposes for cattle and sheep. The most wonderful attraction of the island is that it possesses great numbers of marvelous stone images, huge, sculptured, and of unknown origin.

"A Robinson Crusoe Party"

Adventure calls to all young people, whether it be the old adventures of the past, or the new, untried ways of the future. A party of this kind requires some ingenuity but it is an unusual party idea, and should appeal especially to the longing in all human hearts to "go native". Primitive ways and days are always delightful to read about, and may be turned into a party occasion by using Robinson Crusoe as a basis.

INVITATIONS: Select a correspondence card for the invitations and draw with crayon or ink, a cave on one side of the card, or a rough idea of a shelter. Almost everyone knows the story of Robinson Crusoe and his man, Friday, castaways on an island, and how Robinson Crusoe set up a tent or canvas and piled boxes and chests around it for protection against wild animals. Any kind of a sketch that carries out this idea is appropriate. Then, the words of the invitation should be on this order, in rough, scrawly writing:

> "A Robinson Crusoe party will be held on September twenty-ninth at the home of Albert Trent, Providence Park Road, Friday, at eight-thirty o'clock. Let's "go native" for awhile, and camp around in Crusoe style! Though indoors, we will try this stunt, we'll have a real wild animal hunt!"

DECORATIONS: A Robinson Crusoe party requires a clever setting. Remove as much of the furniture as possible, or convert it into "rocks", "mounds", "caves", and so forth by inverting such things as chairs, small tables, divans, and covering them with brown or green cloth or rugs. Use boxes covered with cloth or rugs in place of chairs, for the guests, also cushions on the floor. In September, leaves, greens, ground pine, laurel, rhododendron, hemlock, real rocks and trees may be used to create a woods effect, in corners especially. Very little else will be necessary unless, possibly, a few wild animals cut out of cardboard and painted, should be placed in dark spots, partly out of sight, to show a little of the wild life of Crusoe's island. Colored birds in the trees might be used. If one of the committee would dress like Crusoe in a pointed fur cap, short fur coat, and short trousers and leggings, gun and all, it would be a good feature as long as he could stand the warmth. Of course a real fur cap and coat could be used, but a costume gotten up for the occasion would be just right to create fun, and could doubtless be made out of cloth with less warmth. Crusoe longed for real shoes to wear but found none in the boat. He wore a sort of fur legging that formed a shoe for his foot. His man, Friday, could wear a suit of imitation fur like Crusoe's, but no hat. Costumes might be removed after the party had progressed awhile. When the guests arrive and have removed their wraps, present each one with the name of a wild animal printed in large letters and pinned to the back securely. All through the party, the guest maintains the part of the wild animal he represents, and must respond at any time with demonstrations of his ability as a wolf, hyena, bear, wild cat, fox, lynx, lion, tiger, jaguar, or ape. Any wild animal name may be used, also male and female types.

GAME—"WHO'S WHO IN WILD ANIMALS"

The first "hunt" should be to get acquainted with the wild animals present both species, tiger and tigress. On cardboard shaped like an animal, in different colors, and with pencils of all kinds and shapes, invite the guests to write the names of as many other guests as they can, each guest trying to avoid being "read" but not allowed to back against any object in the room. Once being able to see the name on the back of a guest, it would be no trouble to jot it down, but the fun is in having a hard time to get some stubborn guest to turn his back toward the player.

No player is permitted to help another, as there are hard penalties for lending assistance, to be paid later in the evening. After sufficient time has been allowed for guessing names, collect the cards and see who has been able to obtain the most names of guests, awarding a prize of peanuts with which to feed the animals! A roll call of guests by the hostess would result in each guest responding to his animal cognomen, with the proper yelp or growl. This starts the party off nicely, though a Robinson Crusoe party is a self-starter because of its novelty of dress, decoration and setting, not to mention "amosphere".

CRUSOE PASTIMES

While the guests are seated, give to the men short round sticks to whittle to a sharp point, either with their own knives or extra ones supplied by the hostess or host. To the girls give loose string to be wound into balls, or a spool of silkateen may be unwound into an envelope, and given to each girl to wind up. The men should each have a newspaper on which to whittle his stick. A time limit is given, and the best point on a stick wins a belt, sort of a gay Robinson Crusoe affair, just in fun. The girl who winds the best ball of silkateen or yarn in the shortest time receives a sewing bag of imitation skin (brown cloth or oilcloth) also her ball of silkateen as a prize.

GAME—"CRUSOE'S CAVE"

Pass large sheets of brown paper and pencils and ask the guests to draw a cave or tent, or perhaps just a shelter such as they think Crusoe might have used. A tent with high fence of stakes and brush and a ladder such as Crusoe used to climb over into his shelter each night is an idea of Crusoe's house on the island. The guests should be told to give their imagination free rein and the drawings should prove a surprise and delight in more ways than one. A prize of a small basket of oranges for the first prize, and a lemon for a consolation prize since these fruits were found on Crusoe's island. All good drawings should be placed on exhibition, but poor attempts should not be exploited at the expense of feelings.

GAME—"INDOOR BOWLING"

If nine pins can be set up indoors, with soft balls for rolling, the game would provide action for awhile. In a hall this would be very possible and if sides or teams are chosen, the interest would be maintained, especially if sides were to be christened "Robinson Crusoe" and "Man Friday". In a home, a variation may be an Indian club set up on a cushion to represent a mound on the island, a player asked to serve as guard, and the players to try to knock down the club with soft rubber balls as many times as possible, scores to be kept for the teams or sides and the guard to decide all arguments and keep the game fair. A test number of feet from the Indian club would determine a fair distance to be lined off. The winning side receives a basket of candy kernels of corn such as may be obtained in any good candy store, and the losing side a cocoanut.

GAME—"ISLAND ANIMALS"

For a game in which the guests may be seated, after the Indian club target contest, an animal game is in order. The players are given questions about animals by the leader, and the first person in the circle of guests tries to give a correct oral answer. He is given a piece of candy. If his answer is correct, he places the candy which is in the form of a nut in a small paper basket he has received; if his answer is wrong, he must eat the candy nut at once! The player having the most nuts in his basket at the end of the game is the winner and receives a stick of gum for every nut as a prize. He may share his winnings if he wishes. The one having the fewest nuts is given a pickled lime as a consolation prize. Sharing goes for this, too, if desired! The questions follow:

1. What animal acts like a young school girl? Coyote.
2. What animal is partly a color? Buffalo.

3. What animal is part wood and part man? Chipmonk.
4. What animal is happy? Gazelle.
5. What animal is untruthful? Lion.
6. What animal wears a neckpiece as men do? Tiger.
7. What animal is part wood and part meat? Woodchuck.
8. What animal is part meat and part tree? Porcupine.
9. What animal is partly a dish? Panther.
10. What animal is the opposite of low? Hyena.
11. What animal is tiny? Weasel.
12. What animal is part of the human body? Hippopotamus.
13. What animal is expensive? Deer.
14. What animal is part of a house? Elephant.
15. What animal is part misery? ·Wolf.

DIVERSIONS: A chest on the table, with slips of paper in it and on them names of articles Robinson Crusoe found in his treasure chest from the wrecked boat, tobacco, Bible, bread, rice, cheese, swords, gun, powder, carpenter's tools, grindstone, men's clothes, hammock, bedding, bullets, nails, saws. Players may guess what Robinson Crusoe had to start life with on the island. Lists may be read to see how near they are to the names on the slips of paper in the chest. No prizes are needed, the diversion only intended to revive the story of Robinson Crusoe.

Following a trail over Crusoe's island, that is, jumping a stream (a yardstick); picking up nuts (split peas); picking fruit from trees (hopping up and reaching high); seeing a savage (crouching low); reaping his fields (swinging from side to side; climbing a hill (stepping up and down in one spot); shooting game (aim! bang!); seeing wild animals (sidestepping); watching birds in trees ('Tweet! tweet!); talking to his dog and patting him. After the diversions, a real game may be played.

GAME—"TARGET PRACTICE"

Have a large circle of cardboard and all the names of the girls upon the circle. Give the men sling shots and wads of paper. Have a sponge in a small dish of water at hand for wetting the wads of paper. Invite the men to shoot at the target and win a partner for the refreshments. The men will enjoy making wet wads to land on the target, and if the target is far enough away, they will find the shooting more difficult and the fair partner harder to win. The girls will use their football fan tactics, and be quite anxious as to the outcome.

REFRESHMENTS: For a Robinson Crusoe party, the refreshments should be all "in the raw" but as that seems a little difficult, try having them served in cafeteria style, the men procuring the trays for their partners, and having unusual dishes to choose from, the menu being as follows— water lily salad on individual plates. This is made of hard boiled eggs, with olives sliced around the flower for green petals, very pretty in effect. Then have baby Parker House rolls buttered and kept warm if possible in covered dishes over hot water. Toasted crackers sprinkled with paprika. Ice cream in moulds of different fruits on spun glass would carry out the idea of the fruits that Crusoe found in plenty on his island. Sponge cake in triangular slices, like a tent in shape, would be attractive, with coffee. If desired, fancy names could be used on the refreshments such as Water Lily Combination, Crusoe Buns, Wild Animal Crackers, Frozen Fruits, Sponge Wedges, and Plant Nectar. While the refreshments are being enjoyed, have Crusoe stroll around with a toy dog, a parrot and two cats, his man Friday bringing up the rear, for all these companions kept Crusoe from going crazy from loneliness. They might work up a few funny stunts, and make a jolly ending to the party, staging a final rescue tableau.

"A Bookland Party"

The name "book" was formed from the Anglo-Saxon words "boc", "bece", meaning "beech" because the Saxons wrote tunes on pieces of beechen board. It has many combinations in modern use, and books have come to mean so much to civilization that life, health, and happiness depends to a great extent on book knowledge and appreciation. Bookland is the opposite of folkland and originally meant land granted by a book or charter. Out of books we learn much and in bookland we wander for many thrills and pleasures. A Bookland Party is one in which we may visit strange lands, see strange faces, and do strange things through the medium of books.

INVITATIONS: The invitations for this kind of a party should be in the form of small folders with leaves like a book. These may be of the store or home-made variety, and if home-made, dark grey cardboard may be obtained in large sheets for ten cents a sheet. Each sheet would make thirty or more small folders or books. White ink may be obtained and the invitations worded as follows on the inside of the folders:

"We are giving a Bookland Party at our home, Number Eight Adams Avenue, on Saturday Evening, at eight o'clock, September Tenth. Please wear some object representing a book, or prepare to act out a book in pantomime. We hope you will be sure to come. The Misses Bertha and Grace Wood."

The outside of these small folders might have a design cut from a magazine and pasted on it, or very pretty colored seals may be bought by the box and these would serve admirably to adorn it. If four leaves are made, tie with class colors in baby ribbon or tinsel cord, but keep the folder from being too bulky for envelopes which should be bought in a grey color to hold folders.

DECORATIONS: For a bookland party, ideas from many books may be used. One corner of a room could be arranged to represent Nature books, using greens of all kinds, stuffed birds and animals, and butterflies made of crepe paper. Another corner could be devoted to Travel books, with China, Japan, Egypt, Africa, France, and England represented by silks; Japanese cherry tree (pink crepe paper tied to tree branches very effective); picture of the Pyramids, Nile, Sphinx, or Cleopatra; pictures of dark men of Africa and jungle scenes; fashion models from France, and England's "bobbies". In a hall, this idea would work out in a striking manner; in a home it may be followed in a general way and provide interest. More simple decorations for a bookland party may be large-sized pictures of authors of books, which doubtless could be obtained in fine sets from the Perry Pictures Company or any local bookstore, or even from magazines. This may be placed about the rooms without names in sight, in vases of artificial flowers, and will provide sufficient decoration for a home party if twenty-five or more are used in artistic arrangement.

GAME—"TOUR INTO BOOLKAND"

If the guests have arrived wearing some object representing a book, or prepared to pantomime a book, a tour into Bookland may begin at once, as a means of friendly conversation. All are provided with pencils and papers and invited to guess the name of the book which each one represents. For instance, Frank Jones with a large red letter on his chest! Miss Evans with a picture of green fields pinned on her shoulder as "Green Pastures"; a black toy horse for "Black Beauty"; a group of small paper dolls for "Little Women", and many other ideas along the same line. By the time all book titles have been guessed approximately, there will be no chance of a slow start, for in the receiving line are characters who have stepped bodily out of books, Anthony Adverse, Great-Aunt Lavina, Hypatia, Uncle Tom, Sara Bessett, Fu Manchu, and others, with all of whom the guests must shake hands and guess whom they represent with so much dignity. The person who guesses the most correct numbers of books represented by guests should be awarded a small gift book, and the one guessing the fewest, a circular of some book publishing house, on which has been fastened a home-made cover—a friendly hint to "study up on books".

GAME—"BOOK TABLEAUS"

The next game should be in the form of dramatizing books, scenes from books, or pantomiming book titles. The guests should be seated for this game, and the performers should be groups, couples and individuals, with the more familiar books and scenes acted out. Romeo and Juliet acted out upon a ladder proves most delightful and funny. The parts may be memorized beforehand or read from script furnished by the hostesses. If no man will rise to be Romeo, then invite a peppy lady guest to dress and act as Romeo, using anything at hand for a costume. The hostesses may have on hand a long list of suggestions and with a little prodding, many of the guests will enjoy trying out their histrionic ability in an amateur audition, just for fun and frolic and in the spirit of co-operation. This game or pastime should continue long enough to discover if there is real talent in the class, or just misplaced ambition! There will be some of both, and all should enjoy the tests, whether Major Bowes is present or not, and whether there is four-star acting or not!

GAME—"FAVORITE BOOK QUIZ"

In this game all guests are comfortably seated and the leader does all the work! Each player is invited to select his or her favorite book and be ready to use it as an answer to the leader's questions. The questions are somewhat as follows:

Leader: "If you were a hermit, what book would you prefer as a companion?" Answer: "Little Women."

Leader: "If you were the president of the United States, what book would you use to help balance the budget?" Answer: "Gone with the Wind."

Leader: "If you were traveling through China, what book would you use as a guide?" Answer: "Almanac."

Other questions may be formulated and the quiz continue until the leader calls for a game with real action.

GAME—"BOOKLAND RACES"

The first race is between two goals, blindfolded and with a book on the head of the player. In some countries objects are frequently carried on the heads, so the players try their luck. An egg is placed on the floor on a piece of paper, and the player is told that the egg is the only obstacle, and he must try and not step on it? As soon as the player is blindfolded, crackers are substituted for the egg, and placed in several spots, so when the player steps on one almost surely, and is aghast at the results of his error, he is relieved of his blindfold and shown what it was that smashed so beautifully under his step! This is one heat of the races. Use other obstacles also.

The next is a partner race, and volunteers are called for, either man and girl, or two of a sex. Hand of one is tied to partner's hand, the two must perform together. Arms may be linked, if preferred, or legs tied, if players are men. The course is to pick up a book, step over eight books in a pile, kneel on a cushion, run, hop, bow, and say "how'd do!", sing America, recite a Mother Goose rhyme, eat a piece of celery. All of this must be done together, and any other stunts the leader suggests to the unfortunate partners. Partners may have book titles on backs.

The last race is to choose sides or arrange teams for a swift blackboard race in forming words. If possible, obtain a large blackboard on a stand, or make a substantial stand for one. If there is a large enough wall space and two strong hooks, it may be hung on the wall. First one side, and then the other, is invited to add a letter to the letters on the blackboard, and the object is to see which

side can form a word of a prescribed number of letters,
first, the longer the word, the harder the game. No erasures
are allowed and there must be a time limit for each letter
to be added. One side begins by writing or printing a letter. Members of each side should take turns, and failure
of any member gives the turn to the other side. Play continues until one side or the other has scored heavily on
words, and that side is awarded a box of candy. The losing
side receives a bag of peanuts.

DIVERSIONS: Lists of words containing the word "book".
Best sentence constructed with the letters "B. O. O. K." List
ten book titles, players to answer with author's names.

GAME—"PROVERBS"

A change from book titles may be to have the players
form a ring and the leader goes round outside the ring
and recites loudly half of an old proverb or saying which
is familiar to everyone, as "Make hay while . . . "; All is
not . . . "; "A bird in the . . . "; "Every cloud has . . . ";
"A stitch in . . . ". The leader drops a handkerchief or taps
a player on the shoulder, and the player must finish the
proverb correctly, and catch and tag the leader, or be "it"
himself. The leader is "spry", and the player must be
"spryer" to catch him before he gets into the circle. A
variation of this game may be for the leader to select combinations of foods such as "pork and beans", "bread and
butter", "ham and eggs", "soup and noodles", and call out
the half of the combination when tagging. The player
tagged must answer loud and snappy with the proper half
and be quick to catch the leader. A player too slow in
answering may be ruled out by a referee, if desired, so
that the game may move in more lively fashion, and be
more fun for all. The combinations for this game may be
used also in partnering the guests for the refreshments, if
desired, passing half to the men and half to the girls, and
asking players to find their "better halves". Another method of partnering for a Bookland Party is to have characters appearing together in bookland such as Othello and
Desdemona, Romeo and Juliet, Uncle Tom and Little Eva,

Jack and Jill, Mutt and Jeff—in fact, almost any similar pairs of names that are most well known, used for the purpose of arranging couples.

REFRESHMENTS: The refreshments for a Bookland Party should be novel in character. Marguerites are small cakes, Brownies are a delicious cake confection, Dutch cake may always be served with coffee, and takes the place of sandwiches very nicely. There are various salads from foreign countries in almost every modern cook book. The idea is to have a varied menu that shall suggest the cooking of other lands. A Bookland Party may have the refreshments served from card tables, each table representing a foreign land and its cookery, Japanese eggs, German salad, Dutch cake, French Madeleines, Chinese tea, English muffins, American ices, Turkish coffee. All these suggestions may be appropriately used at each small table, the service being either cafeteria or waitress style. If a dining room table is used, write on each place card the name of a foreign author, either prose writer or poet. The menu should consist of sandwiches in many different shapes but very small; tiny cream cheese balls; Washington cream pie, and coffee. If conversation requires stimulation, the hostesses should ask each guest to tell in what way he thinks he himself resembles the distinguished author written on his card at his place! The Bookland Party should close with the singing of any well-known songs of other countries, class songs, or "America, The Beautiful",—the home of the "Best Seller", and many Nobel Prize winners.